Contemporary

European

Architects

Volume IV

Philip Jodidio

Contemporary **European** Architects

Volume IV

TASCHEN

KÖLN LISBOA LONDON NEW YORK PARIS TOKYO

In Praise of the Newly Modern
European Architects in the 1990s

Das Hohelied der neuen Moderne
Europäische Architekten in den 90er Jahren

Eloge des nouveaux modernes
Architectes européens des années 90

Although no critic has rushed forward to give recent architecture a name, it is clear that the time of the Post-Modern is gone. Modernism in its anti-historical incarnation ebbed slowly throughout the 1960s and 1970s, to be challenged by architects who joyfully dressed their largely conventional buildings with bright colors, false columns and Italianate windows. Michael Graves, Robert A.M. Stern or Charles Moore in the United States, Ricardo Bofill in Europe were leading figures of what one critic called "Supermannerism," but what might better have been named "facadism." A dictionary definition of the word "facade" is "a superficial appearance or illusion of something." Indeed, despite a rhetoric which claimed deep kinship most notably with the Baroque or Mannerist past, Post-Modernism might best be symbolized by Philip Johnson's imposing AT&T Building on Madison Avenue in New York, designed in 1978. Here a stone facade with a "Chippendale" flourish at the top was hailed as a brilliant rupture with the past. "The 'modern' hated history, we love it. The 'modern' hated symbols, we love them. The 'modern' built in the same way no matter what the location, we seek out the spirit of a place, the *genius loci*, for inspiration and for variety," said Philip Johnson in his acceptance speech for the 1978 American Institute of Architects (AIA) Gold Medal. Few critics at the time called attention to the fact that behind its facade the AT&T Building was much like any other midtown Manhattan skyscraper.

It remains that 1970s Post-Modernism opened the way for a reevaluation of the rapport between contemporary architecture and the historical past. Facadism of a sort is still very much in style, although the avowed preoccupation of some architects is with what they now call the "skin" of a building. That said, after a marked rejection of the strict geometric forms of the Modernist or International Style, architects have come almost full circle, realizing that pastiche can not fundamentally ameliorate the viability of a structure, they have dared to attempt to reconcile the distant past and more recent modern tradition. Approaching a sensitive historical site like that of his Galician Center for Contemporary Art, in Santiago de Compostela, Spain,

Page 6: *Alvaro Siza, Galician Center for Contemporary Art, Santiago de Compostela, Spain, 1988–95. Interior view.*

Seite 6: *Alvaro Siza, Galizisches Zentrum für zeitgenössische Kunst, Santiago de Compostela, Spanien, 1988–95. Innenansicht.*

Page 6: *Alvaro Siza, Centre galicien d'art contemporain, Saint-Jacques-de-Compostelle, Espagne, 1988–95. Vue intérieure.*

Obwohl noch kein Kritiker den Versuch unternommen hat, der zeitgenössischen Architektur einen Namen zu verleihen, ist die Zeit der Postmoderne zweifellos vorüber. Während der 60er und 70er Jahre ebbte die Moderne in ihrer anti-historischen Inkarnation langsam ab und wurde von Architekten in Frage gestellt, die ihre zumeist konventionellen Gebäude fröhlich mit leuchtenden Farben, falschen Säulen und italianisierten Fenstern ausstatteten. Michael Graves, Robert A.M. Stern und Charles Moore in den Vereinigten Staaten oder Ricardo Bofill in Europa galten als Vorreiter einer Entwicklung, die ein Kritiker als »Supermanierismus« bezeichnete, die aber eher den Namen »Fassadismus« hätte tragen sollen. Das Wörterbuch definiert den Begriff »Fassade« als »oberflächliches Erscheinungsbild oder Illusion eines Objekts, das über das eigentliche Wesen nichts aussagt«. Und tatsächlich – trotz einer Stilistik, die eine enge Verwandtschaft mit der barocken oder manieristischen Vergangenheit geltend machte, ist die Postmoderne wahrscheinlich am besten in Philip Johnsons eindrucksvollem AT&T (American Telephone and Telegraph) Building symbolisiert, das 1978 an der New Yorker Madison Avenue entstand. Eine steinerne Fassade mit einem »Chippendale«-Schnörkel als Aufsatz wurde als brillanter Bruch mit der Vergangenheit bejubelt. »Die ›Moderne‹ haßte die Geschichte, wir lieben sie. Die ›Moderne‹ haßte Symbole, wir lieben sie. Die ›Moderne‹ baute an den verschiedensten Orten immer auf die gleiche Weise, wir suchen den Geist eines Ortes, den *genius loci*, als Inspiration und Abwechslung«, sagte Philip Johnson in seiner Dankesrede anläßlich der Verleihung der Goldmedaille des American Institute of Architects (AIA) 1978. Zu dieser Zeit machten nur wenige Kritiker auf die Tatsache aufmerksam, daß sich das AT&T Building hinter seiner Fassade auch nicht wesentlich von anderen Wolkenkratzern Manhattans unterschied.

Dennoch bleibt unbestritten, daß die Postmoderne der 70er Jahre den Weg für eine Neubewertung des Verhältnisses von zeitgenössischer Architektur und historischer Vergangenheit ebnete. Ein gewisser »Fassadismus« steht immer noch hoch im Kurs, trotz der offen eingestandenen Faszination einiger

Bien qu'aucun critique ne se soit empressé de trouver un terme pour désigner l'architecture de ces dernières années, il est clair que l'ère postmoderne est terminée. Dans son incarnation anti-historique, le modernisme a progressivement perdu du terrain au cours des années 1960 et 1970, pour être finalement contesté par des architectes qui ont allègrement paré leurs bâtiments – pour la plupart conventionnels – de couleurs vives, de fausses colonnes et de fenêtres à l'italienne. Michael Graves, Robert A.M. Stern et Charles Moore aux Etats-Unis, ainsi que Ricardo Bofill en Europe, ont été les plus éminents représentants de ce qu'un critique a qualifié de «supermaniérisme», alors que le terme «façadisme» aurait peut-être mieux convenu. Un dictionnaire propose comme définition du mot «façade»: «apparence superficielle ou illusion de quelque chose». En effet, en dépit d'un discours affirmant ses profondes affinités avec le baroque et le maniérisme, le postmodernisme trouve probablement sa meilleure illustration dans l'imposante AT&T (American Telephone and Telegraph) Building conçue en 1978 par Philip Johnson et située sur Madison Avenue, à New York. Sa façade en pierre, surmontée de fioritures «Chippendale», a été saluée comme une brillante rupture avec le passé. «Les ‹Modernes› détestaient les symboles; nous les adorons. Les ‹Modernes› construisaient de la même manière quel que soit l'emplacement; nous cherchons à capter l'esprit de chaque lieu, le *genius loci*, pour trouver l'inspiration et la diversité», a expliqué Philip Johnson dans son discours lorsqu'il a reçu en 1978 la médaille d'or de l'American Institute of Architects (AIA). A l'époque, rares furent les critiques qui attirèrent l'attention sur le fait que, derrière sa façade, le AT&T Building n'était pas bien différent de n'importe quel autre gratte-ciel du centre de Manhattan.

Il reste cependant indéniable que le postmodernisme des années 1970 a permis de réévaluer les affinités existantes entre l'architecture contemporaine et le passé. Un certain façadisme demeure très à l'honneur, même si quelques architectes affirment se préoccuper de ce qu'ils appellent aujourd'hui la «peau» du bâtiment. Cela dit, après un net rejet des formes géométriques strictes du style moderniste ou international, les

the Portuguese architect Alvaro Siza, for example, has sought out a profound relation between his very contemporary design and the traditional environment. "I have the pretension to say that it refers to the entire history of the city and not only to its own time," says Siza about the Galician Center for Contemporary Art. "This results not from a removal of historical references, but of an attempt at creating a synthesis," concludes the 1992 Pritzker Prize winner.

It seems obvious that European architects are well placed in a creative environment which seeks to bring forth a synthesis between the past and the present. The superficiality of historical references in the Post-Modern period was, after all, due in large part to the removal of American architects from their own deeper (European) historical roots. American architectural history is made up of styles with names like "Neo-Renaissance," or "Neo-Gothic." From Hollywood to Main Street, USA in the heart of Disneyland, facades of various types seek to conjure up images of a missing past. Some American architects, like Richard Meier with his Ulm Exhibition and Assembly Building or Hague City Hall have faced the challenge of a truly historical environment, others are currently looking even further back, to the rich geological history of the American continent. The European architects chosen for this volume are undoubtedly conscious that both the roots of architectural history reaching back to Greece and Rome, and the sources of the modern adventure in pre-War Germany, Holland or Russia are theirs to claim. In this respect, they are once again in the vanguard of world architecture, after a hiatus which might well be related to the lengthy trauma of war and reconstruction.

Museums between the Past and the Future
Born in Milan in 1931, Aldo Rossi is a singular figure most often associated with a Post-Modern vision of architecture. The image of his floating "Teatro del Mondo" completed for the 1980 Venice Biennale comes almost immediately to mind, although the rather funerary, windowless facade of the "Il Palazzo" Hotel in Fukuoka (1990) is now almost as well known. The jury citation

Architekten für das, was sie heute als »Haut« eines Gebäudes bezeichnen. Nach der deutlichen Ablehnung der strengen geometrischen Formen der Moderne und des International Style sind die Architekten fast zum Ausgangspunkt zurückgekehrt. Sie wurden sich der Tatsache bewußt, daß ein Pastiche die Eigenständigkeit eines Bauwerks nicht grundlegend verbessert, und wagten den Versuch einer Aussöhnung vergangener Traditionen mit zeitgenössischen modernen Baustilen. Der portugiesische Architekt Alvaro Siza beispielsweise suchte in seinem Umgang mit einem historisch sensiblen Baugelände wie dem des Galizischen Zentrums für zeitgenössische Kunst (Galician Center for Contemporary Art) in Santiago de Compostela nach einer engen Beziehung zwischen seinem sehr modernen Entwurf und dessen traditionsreicher Umgebung. »Ich habe den Anspruch, daß es mit der gesamten Stadtgeschichte und nicht nur mit seiner eigenen Zeit in Verbindung stehen soll«, sagt Siza über sein Bauwerk. »Diese Verbindung entsteht nicht durch das Weglassen historischer Bezüge, sondern aus dem Versuch einer Synthese«, so der Gewinner des Pritzker Preises 1992.

Offensichtlich fühlen sich europäische Architekten in einem kreativen Umfeld besonders wohl, das eine Synthese aus Vergangenheit und Gegenwart zu schaffen versucht. Die Oberflächlichkeit der historischen Zitate zur Zeit der Postmoderne war größtenteils in der Entfremdung amerikanischer Architekten von ihren eigenen, tieferen (europäischen) Wurzeln begründet. Die amerikanische Architekturgeschichte besteht aus Stilrichtungen wie »Neo-Renaissance« oder »Neo-Gothik«. Von Hollywood bis hin zur Main Street im Herzen von Disneyland, beschwören die verschiedensten Fassaden Bilder einer fehlenden Vergangenheit herauf. Einige amerikanische Architekten, wie Richard Meier mit seinem Stadthaus in Ulm oder dem Den Haager Rathaus, haben sich den Herausforderungen einer gewachsenen historischen Umgebung gestellt; andere blicken zur Zeit noch weiter zurück und befassen sich mit der faszinierenden geologischen Geschichte des amerikanischen Kontinents. Die in diesem Buch vorgestellten europäischen Architekten sind sich der Tatsache bewußt, daß sich einerseits die Wurzeln ihrer architektonischen

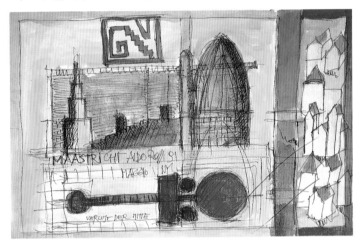

architectes sont presque revenus au point de départ. Se rendant
compte que le pastiche ne peut améliorer fondamentalement la
viabilité d'une structure, ils n'ont pas hésité à essayer de récon-
cilier le passé lointain et la tradition moderne plus récente.

Ainsi, au cours de son travail d'approche d'un site historique
aussi sensible que celui occupé par son Centre galicien d'art
contemporain de Saint-Jacques-de-Compostelle (Espagne),
l'architecte portugais Alvaro Siza, par exemple, a cherché à créer
une relation profonde entre son projet très contemporain et
l'environnement traditionnel. «J'ai la prétention d'affirmer qu'il
fait référence à toute l'histoire de la ville, et pas uniquement à
l'époque de sa propre construction», explique Siza à propos du
Centre galicien d'art contemporain. Et le lauréat du prix Pritzker
1992 de conclure: «Ceci résulte non pas de l'effacement de
toute référence historique, mais d'une tentative de créer une
synthèse.»

De toute évidence, les architectes européens ont la chance de
travailler dans un environnement créatif qui cherche à faire
naître une synthèse entre passé et présent. Après tout, durant la
période postmoderne, le caractère superficiel des références
historiques était essentiellement dû au fait que les architectes
américains étaient loin de leurs racines les plus profondes,
restées en Europe. L'histoire architecturale américaine s'articule
autour de styles désignés par des termes tels que «néo-renais-
sance» ou «néo-gothique». De Hollywood à Main Street, USA,
au cœur de Disneyland, des façades aux styles divers s'efforcent
de faire surgir les images d'un passé nostalgique. Quelques
architectes américains, tel Richard Meier avec son Stadthaus à
Ulm ou son hôtel de ville de La Haye, ont relevé le défi que représente un véritable environnement historique; d'autres remon-
tent aujourd'hui encore plus loin dans le temps, jusqu'aux plus
anciennes richesses géologiques du continent américain. Les
architectes européens évoqués dans ce tome sont sans aucun
doute conscients qu'ils sont en droit de revendiquer comme
leurs aussi bien les racines architecturales remontant à la Grèce
et à la Rome antiques que les sources de l'aventure architecturale moderne d'avant-guerre en Allemagne, aux Pays-Bas et en

*Aldo Rossi, Bonnefanten Museum, Maastricht,
The Netherlands, 1990–94. View of the zinc-covered
dome.*

*Aldo Rossi, Bonnefanten Museum, Maastricht,
Niederlande, 1990–94. Ansicht der zinkverkleideten
Kuppel.*

*Aldo Rossi, musée Bonnefanten, Maastricht,
Pays-Bas, 1990–94. Vue du dôme couvert de zinc.*

for the Pritzker Prize which Rossi won in 1990 does much to
explain the appeal of his work: "Rossi has been able to follow
the lessons of classical architecture without copying them; his
buildings carry echoes from the past in their use of forms that
have a universal, haunting quality. His work is at once bold and
ordinary, original without being novel, refreshingly simple in
appearance, but extremely complex in content and meaning. In a
period of diverse styles and influences, Aldo Rossi has eschewed
the fashionable and popular to create an architecture singularly
his own." By 1990, Rossi like others had begun to shift the
nature of his historical references toward a more subtle and
profound vocabulary, while retaining idiosyncratic references
such as his curious passion for tea pots. Indeed, the tea service
he designed for Alessi in 1980, bears more than a passing
resemblance to the zinc-clad dome of his 1990–94 Bonnefanten
Museum in Maastricht, The Netherlands.

The Bonnefanten Museum, situated on the opposite side
of the Maas River from the old city of Maastricht is at the edge
of a 20 hectare redevelopment zone in the so-called Ceramiqueterrein. The reference to ceramics concerns the factory buildings
which existed previously near this site, and to the newly restored
Wiebengahal. Designed in 1912 by Gerko Wiebenga, this was
the first reinforced concrete building erected in The Netherlands.
The provincial government of Limburg decided to erect the new
Bonnefanten Museum in 1989, setting aside a budget of 40
million florins. Construction started in June 1992, and was
completed in November 1994, leading to an opening on March
11, 1995. A symmetrical E-shaped building with the 28 meter high
dome at its center, the museum is a 6,000 m² structure clad
with Dutch bricks, irish limestone, trachite rosso from Sardinia,

Vergangenheit bis in die griechische und römische Antike erstrecken, und daß sie sich andererseits auf die Abenteuer der Moderne berufen können, deren Ursprünge im Vorkriegsdeutschland, in den Niederlanden und in Rußland liegen. In dieser Hinsicht stehen sie erneut an der Spitze der Architekturwelt – nach einer Unterbrechung, die mit dem langanhaltenden Trauma des Krieges und des Wiederaufbaus zusammenhängen könnte.

Museen zwischen Vergangenheit und Gegenwart

Der 1931 in Mailand geborene Aldo Rossi gilt als einer der am häufigsten mit einer postmodernen Sichtweise in Verbindung gebrachten Architekten. Das Bild seines schwimmenden »Teatro del Mondo«, das Rossi 1980 für die Biennale in Venedig erbaute, taucht sofort vor dem inneren Auge auf, obwohl die düstere, fensterlose Fassade des »Il Palazzo«-Hotels in Fukuoka (1990) heute fast ebenso bekannt ist. Die Jury des Pritzker Preises 1990 erläuterte die Anziehungskraft seiner Arbeiten: »Rossi gelingt es, die Lehren der klassischen Architektur zu befolgen, ohne sie zu kopieren. Die Formensprache seiner Gebäude trägt Bilder der Vergangenheit in sich, die eine universelle und unvergeßliche Qualität besitzen. Seine Arbeiten sind zugleich kühn und gewöhnlich, einzigartig, ohne neuartig zu erscheinen, erfrischend schlicht in ihrem Erscheinungsbild, aber extrem komplex in Aussage und Bedeutung. In einer Zeit unterschiedlicher Stilrichtungen und Einflüsse vermeidet Aldo Rossi alles Modische und Populäre und schafft dabei eine einzigartige, persönliche Architektur.« Ab 1990 hatte Rossi – neben anderen – damit begonnen, die Art seiner historischen Zitate in Richtung auf ein subtileres, tiefsinnigeres Vokabular zu verschieben, während er zugleich typische Merkmale wie seine kuriose Begeisterung für Teekannen beibehielt. In der Tat weist sein 1980 für Alessi entworfenes Teeservice mehr als eine zufällige Ähnlichkeit mit der zinkverkleideten Kuppel des Bonnefanten Museums auf, das er 1990–94 in Maastricht erbaute.

Das Bonnefanten Museum, gegenüber der Maastrichter Altstadt am Maasufer gelegen, entstand am Rand eines 20 Hektar großen Sanierungsgebietes, des sogenannten Ceramiqueterrein.

Russie. A cet égard, ils se situent une fois encore à l'avant-garde de l'architecture mondiale, après une interruption qui pourrait bien être la conséquence du long traumatisme de la guerre puis de la reconstruction.

Des musées entre passé et futur

Né à Milan en 1931, Aldo Rossi est une personnalité originale, la plupart du temps associée à une vision architecturale postmoderne. L'image de son «Teatro del Mondo» flottant, achevé pour la Biennale de Venise 1980, vient presque immédiatement à l'esprit, même si la façade aveugle et plutôt lugubre de l'hôtel «Il Palazzo» de Fukuoka (1990) est aujourd'hui presque aussi célèbre. En 1990, quand Rossi reçoit le prix Pritzker, le commentaire du jury met bien en lumière l'intérêt que suscite son travail: «Rossi a su s'inspirer des leçons de l'architecture classique sans pour autant les copier. Ses bâtiments évoquent le passé par l'utilisation de formes d'une qualité universelle et obsédante. Son œuvre est à la fois osée et quelconque, originale sans innover, rafraîchissante par sa simplicité apparente, mais extrêmement complexe par son contenu et sa signification. A une époque où se côtoient influences et styles divers, Aldo Rossi a su éviter toute concession à la mode et créer une architecture singulièrement personnelle.» Avant même 1990, comme d'autres, Rossi avait commencé à modifier ses références historiques pour adopter un vocabulaire plus subtil et plus profond, tout en conservant des sources d'inspiration très personnelles telles que sa curieuse passion pour les théières. D'ailleurs, le service à thé créé en 1980 pour Alexis et le dôme recouvert de zinc du musée Bonnefanten (1990–94) à Maastricht (Pays-Bas), ont plus qu'une vague ressemblance.

Le musée Bonnefanten est situé au bord de la Meuse, sur la rive opposée à la vieille ville de Maastricht. Il s'élève en bordure d'une zone de réaménagement de 20 hectares, sur le site dénommé Ceramiqueterrein. Cette allusion à la céramique fait référence à la fois à l'usine qui occupait autrefois l'emplacement voisin et au Wiebengahal récemment rénové. Celui-ci, conçu par Gerko Wiebenga en 1912, fut le premier bâtiment en béton armé

iron, and zinc for the cupola. Like many Dutch museums, the Bonnefanten houses a heterogeneous group of works including local archeological finds, and contemporary art. It was conceived by Rossi as a response to museum director Alexander van Grevenstein's description of "a place where the visitor has to pause a moment... an impressive spatial gesture, which serves to remind people where they are." The 3,000 m² Wiebengahal now serves as an annex to the museum, containing site-specific installations of contemporary sculpture.

With its austere brick walls and rough Malaysian timber board floors, the Maastricht museum seems to be the antithesis of the colorful exuberance seen in Alessandro Mendini's 1994 Groninger Museum, also in The Netherlands. Indeed, both institutions are witnesses to the remarkable openness of the Dutch toward modern art and architecture. Both at the official level and at that of the public, there is a genuine interest in and appreciation for the contemporary which some other European countries would do well to contemplate.

Imbued with a sense of its relation to the former industrial environment of the Ceramiqueterrein, and naturally to the neighboring Wiebengahal, the Bonnefanten Museum demonstrates a respect both for its location, and for the works of art which are displayed in a straightforward, agreeable way.

Although Aldo Rossi's sources in Maastricht lie principally in the tradition of industrial architecture, he remains aware of the neighboring, and much older city. Reference to the distant past was not a necessary element in the concept of the Kunstmuseum Wolfsburg , in Wolfsburg, Germany. In 1937, this community, located in Lower Saxony, was no more than a village. The following year, the headquarters of the automobile company Volkswagen opened there. With a 1994 population of 129,000, Wolfsburg is a "company town." Indeed, the new Kunstmuseum was financed by the Volkswagen Art Foundation, established in 1987. Despite the relative "youth" of Wolfsburg, the architect Peter Schweger did have to come to terms with two prestigious modern neighbors, Alvar Aalto's 1962 Kulturzentrum and Hans Scharoun's 1973 theater. Situated on an axis, or in what the

Der Name des Geländes bezieht sich auf die Gebäude einer keramischen Fabrik, die ursprünglich in der Nähe des heutigen Museums standen, sowie auf die neu restaurierte Wiebengahal. Bei dieser 1912 von Gerko Wiebenga entworfenen Halle handelt es sich um den ersten Stahlbetonbau der Niederlande. 1989 beschloß die Regierung der Provinz Limburg den Bau des neuen Bonnefanten Museums und stellte dafür einen Etat von 40 Millionen Gulden zur Verfügung. Die Bauzeit dauerte von Juni 1992 bis November 1994; die offizielle Eröffnung fand am 11. März 1995 statt. Dieser symmetrische, E-förmige Bau, in dessen Mitte eine 28 Meter hohe Kuppel aufragt, ist ein 6000 m² großes Gebäude, verkleidet mit holländischen Ziegeln, irischem Kalkstein, rotem Trachit aus Sardinien sowie Eisen und Zink für die Kuppel. Rossi entwarf den Museumsbau als Reaktion auf die Beschreibung des Museumsdirektors Alexander van Grevenstein, der »einen Ort [suchte], an dem der Besucher einen Moment verweilen muß... eine beeindruckende räumliche Geste, die den einzelnen daran erinnert, wo er sich befindet.« Die 3000 m² große Wiebengahal dient heute als Museumsanbau und zeigt ortsgebundene Installationen zeitgenössischer Bildhauerkunst.

Mit nüchternen Ziegelwänden und rauhen Böden aus malaysischem Holz wirkt das Maastrichter Museum wie die Antithese zur farbenfrohen Überschwenglichkeit des von Alessandro Mendini 1994 entworfenen Groninger Museums. Aber letztendlich zeugen beide Institutionen von der bemerkenswerten Offenheit der Niederlande gegenüber moderner Kunst und Architektur. Sowohl auf offizieller Ebene als auch seitens der Öffentlichkeit besteht ein ernsthaftes Interesse und eine Aufgeschlossenheit gegenüber zeitgenössischen Tendenzen.

Erfüllt von einem Gefühl der Verbundenheit zum früheren industriellen Umfeld des Ceramiqueterrein – und natürlich zur benachbarten Wiebengahal – zollt das Bonnefanten Museum sowohl seinem Standort als auch den hier gezeigten Kunstwerken Respekt, die auf unkomplizierte, ansprechende Weise präsentiert werden.

Obwohl Aldo Rossi in Maastricht hauptsächlich Bezüge zur

construit aux Pays-Bas. C'est en 1989 que le gouvernement de la province de Limbourg décida de construire le nouveau musée Bonnefanten, auquel fut affecté un budget de 40 millions de florins. La construction commença en juin 1992 pour s'achever en novembre 1994. L'inauguration eut lieu le 11 mars 1995. Le dôme, haut de 28 mètres, occupe le centre d'un bâtiment symétrique, en forme de E. Cette structure, qui s'étend sur 6000 m², est habillée de briques hollandaises, de calcaire irlandais, de trachite rosso de Sardaigne et de fer, tandis que la coupole est couverte de zinc. Comme beaucoup de musées néerlandais, le Bonnefanten abrite un ensemble hétérogène comprenant des découvertes archéologiques locales ainsi que des œuvres d'art contemporain. Rossi l'a conçu comme une réponse à la description du conservateur, Alexander van Grevenstein, qui conçoit ce musée comme «un lieu où le visiteur vient faire une pause, l'espace d'un instant... un geste spatial impressionnant, qui sert à rappeler aux gens où ils se trouvent». Aujourd'hui, les 3000 m² du Wiebengahal servent d'annexe au musée et abritent des installations de sculpture contemporaine spécifiques au site.

L'austérité de ses murs de brique et l'aspect brut des planchers en bois de Malaisie font de ce musée l'antithèse de l'exubérance colorée d'un autre musée néerlandais, celui de Groningue, conçu par Alessandro Mendini. De fait, les deux institutions témoignent de la remarquable ouverture d'esprit des Néerlandais vis-à-vis de l'art et de l'architecture modernes. Tant au niveau officiel que dans la population, la création contemporaine suscite un véritable intérêt et une compréhension que certains autres pays européens feraient bien de méditer.

Riche du rapport établi avec l'ancien environnement du Ceramiqueterrein et avec le Wiebengahal tout proche, le musée Bonnefanten respecte son emplacement, mais aussi les œuvres qui y sont exposées de manière simple et agréable.

A Maastricht, tout en s'inspirant de l'architecture industrielle traditionnelle, Aldo Rossi a tenu compte de la ville voisine, bien plus ancienne. En revanche, pour le Kunstmuseum de Wolfsburg (Allemagne), il n'était pas nécessaire de faire référence au passé

Schweger + Partner, Kunstmuseum Wolfsburg, Wolfsburg, Germany, 1989–93. The roof structure extends beyond the building to convey a feeling of openness.

Schweger + Partner, Kunstmuseum Wolfsburg, Wolfsburg, Deutschland, 1989–93. Die Dachkonstruktion erstreckt sich über das Gebäude hinaus und erzeugt so den Eindruck von Offenheit und Weite.

Schweger + Partner, Kunstmuseum de Wolfsburg, Allemagne, 1989–93. La structure du toit se prolonge par une vaste avancée qui accentue le côté aérien du bâtiment.

Alvaro Siza, Galician Center for Contemporary Art, Santiago de Compostela, Spain, 1988–95. An intimate rapport between the old and the new.

Alvaro Siza, Galizisches Zentrum für zeitgenössische Kunst, Santiago de Compostela, Spanien, 1988–95. Eine harmonische Beziehung von Altem und Neuem.

Alvaro Siza, Centre galicien d'art contemporain, Saint-Jacques-de-Compostelle, Espagne, 1988–95. Une rencontre intime entre l'ancien et le nouveau.

architect calls a "field of tension" between these monuments, the Kunstmuseum is part of an urban master plan, which together with a city hall extension is intended to "reinterpret the southern entrance to the city center in relation to the existing buildings." Schweger's elegant solution is a geometric design with a soaring 18.8 meter high roof, "a kind of urban loggia," with an entrance in the form of a 16.8 meter high rotunda, situated at the northwest corner. Steel, aluminum and glass are used in such a way as to conserve the impression of great lightness imparted by the extending roof. The use of the same granite pavement on the external piazza and in the foyer area accentuates the feeling of continuity and free passage which is naturally implicit in the definition of the building as a gateway to the city. Light and space are the essential elements which distinguish this structure, conceived with a rigorous 8.10 x 8.10 meter primary grid from a Modernism which feigned to ignore its environment. This museum is both open and respectful of its context.

Alvaro Siza, born in Porto, Portugal in 1933 first gained recognition for small projects built near his native city, but since receiving the European Economic Community's Mies van der Rohe prize in 1988 and the Pritzker Prize in 1992, he has been considered a figure of international importance. Although it is located very close to Porto, Santiago de Compostela has offered Siza an occasion to reconfirm his standing with his first museum commission. Situated within the boundaries of the former orchard of the 17th century Convent of Santo Domingo de Boneval and bounded by the Valle-Inclan square, the site of the Galician Center for Contemporary Art is intimately related

Tradition der Industriearchitektur herstellte, blieb er sich der benachbarten, wesentlich älteren Stadt durchaus bewußt. Solche Auseinandersetzungen mit der Vergangenheit waren bei der Konzeption des Kunstmuseums Wolfsburg nicht notwendig. Noch 1937 war diese niedersächsische Gemeinde nicht mehr als ein Dorf; erst im Jahr darauf wurde hier der Hauptsitz des Automobilherstellers Volkswagen eröffnet. 1994 zählte Wolfsburg 129000 Einwohner – eine typische »Firmenstadt«, deren neues Kunstmuseum von der 1987 gegründeten Volkswagen Kunststiftung finanziert wurde. Trotz der relativen »Jugend« Wolfsburgs mußte sich der Architekt Peter Schweger bei seinem Entwurf mit zwei renommierten modernen »Nachbarn« auseinandersetzen, Alvar Aaltos 1962 entstandenem Kulturzentrum und Hans Scharouns 1973 erbautem Stadttheater. In einem »Spannungsfeld« zwischen diesen Bauwerken gelegen, ist das Kunstmuseum Teil eines urbanen Bebauungsplans, der zusammen mit einer Erweiterung des Rathauses »den südlichen Zugang zum Stadtzentrum im Verhältnis zu den bereits existierenden Bauten neu interpretieren soll«. Schwegers elegante Lösung ist ein geometrischer Entwurf mit einem schwebenden, 18,8 Meter hohen Dach, »eine Art urbaner Loggia« mit einer 16,8 Meter hohen Rotunde als Eingang an der Nordwestecke des Gebäudes. Durch die Verwendung von Stahl, Aluminium und Glas wird der Eindruck großer Leichtigkeit erzeugt, der sich auch in dem vorspringenden Dach fortsetzt. Die gleichartige Granitpflasterung sowohl auf dem Platz vor dem Gebäude als auch im Foyer verstärkt das Gefühl der Kontinuität und der freien Durchgängigkeit, die der Definition des Kunstmuseums als Eingangstor zur Stadt zugrundeliegt. Licht und Raum sind die grundlegenden Bestandteile dieser Konstruktion, die in einem strengen Raster von 8,10 m x 8,10 m entworfen wurde – ganz im Stil einer Moderne, die vorgibt, ihre Umgebung zu ignorieren. Das Museum ist zugleich offen und voller Respekt gegenüber seinem architektonischen Kontext.

Seit dem Gewinn des Mies van der Rohe-Preises der Europäischen Gemeinschaft 1988 sowie des Pritzker Preises 1992 gilt der Portugiese Alvaro Siza als Architekt von internationalem

lointain. En 1937, cette communauté de Basse-Saxe n'était qu'un village. L'année suivante, le siège social de la firme automobile Volkswagen s'y installe. En 1994, avec ses 129000 habitants, Wolfsburg est devenue une véritable «ville d'entreprise». De fait, le Kunstmuseum a été financé par la Fondation Volkswagen, créée en 1987. Même si Wolksburg est relativement «jeune», l'architecte Peter Schweger a dû tenir compte de l'existence de deux voisins modernes et prestigieux: le Kulturzentrum d'Alvar Aalto construit en 1962, ainsi que le théâtre de Hans Scharoun conçu en 1973. Situé sur un axe, ou plutôt à l'intérieur de ce que l'architecte présente comme un «champ de tension» entre ces deux ouvrages imposants, le Kunstmuseum fait partie d'un plan d'urbanisme général. L'ensemble constitué par le musée et une annexe de l'hôtel de ville est destiné à «redéfinir l'entrée sud de la ville par rapport aux bâtiments existants». La solution élégante proposée par Schweger consiste en un bâtiment géométrique dont le toit s'élève à 18,8 mètres, «une sorte de loggia urbaine» dont l'entrée en rotonde, haute de 16,8 mètres, se situe à l'angle nord-ouest. L'acier, l'aluminium et le verre renforcent l'impression de grande légèreté créée par la hauteur du toit. Le fait d'utiliser le même dallage en granit pour la place extérieure et le foyer accentue l'impression de continuité et de liberté de circulation inhérente à la définition du bâtiment en tant que porte d'accès à la ville. La lumière et l'espace sont les principaux éléments de cette structure, conçue à partir d'un quadrillage de base strict de 8,10 x 8,10 mètres inspiré d'un modernisme qui prétendait ignorer son environnement. Ce musée est à la fois ouvert et respectueux de son contexte. Né à Porto en 1933, Alvaro Siza s'est d'abord fait connaître par de modestes projets réalisés près de sa ville natale. Depuis qu'il a reçu le prix Mies van der Rohe de la Communauté économique européenne en 1988 et le prix Pritzker en 1992, il a acquis une stature internationale. Bien que très proche de Porto, Saint-Jacques-de-Compostelle a permis à Siza de confirmer sa réputation en lui commandant son premier musée. Situé à l'intérieur de l'ancien verger du couvent de Santo Domingo de Boneval datant du XVIIe siècle, et donnant sur la place Valle-Inclan, l'emplacement occupé par le Centre galicien

to a larger area including the Convent of San Roque, the Camino Gateway and the houses situated between As Rodas Street and Valle-Inclan Street. Emerging from the hillside the granite facades of the museum do somehow achieve the delicate balance between past and present sought by the architect. As he has said, "The facades of the museum are monumental because they have almost no windows. Because of their lack of detail, they can achieve a strength which is equal to that of the church or the convent. Within, the museum does not suggest an itinerary to the visitor, but rather a series of alternatives. One of our problems with this project was that at the beginning, there was neither a collection nor a curator. Our only choice was to offer a flexible system, permitting various different types of use."[1] In the context of contemporary museum construction it may be interesting to note that Siza made a considerable effort to hide the necessary technical systems (security, ventilation and light) in a suspended ceiling, avoiding visible spot lights which he does not favor, and creating the atmosphere of "purity" which he sought.

The erosion of economies such as those of France and Germany is responsible for a slowing in the pace of construction of new museums in those countries. England, which long envied the cultural interventionism of Mitterrand's France today finds itself on the verge of creating a new series of artistically oriented projects. This is because funds from the very successful National Lottery are being set aside for this purpose. In all likelihood, through this method, money will be raised for a number of interesting projects, including Norman Foster's ambitious plan for expansion of the British Museum into the courtyard around the Round Reading Room liberated by the departure of the British Library.

The Swiss architects Herzog & de Meuron were selected in April 1994 to design the new Tate Gallery of Modern Art in London's abandoned Bankside Power Station, just across the Thames from Saint Paul's Cathedral. Destined to contain at least 12.000 m² of gallery space, this new project will be financed – partially through Britain's Millennium Fund, which depends

Rang, und sein erster Museumsauftrag in Santiago de Compostela bot ihm die Gelegenheit, diesen Ruf zu bestätigen. Das Galizische Zentrum für zeitgenössische Kunst liegt auf dem Gelände des ehemaligen Obstgartens des im 17. Jahrhundert gegründeten Klosters Santo Domingo de Bonaval.

Sizas Bauwerk steht in enger Beziehung zu einem größeren Areal, zu dem das Convento de San Roque, die Puerta del Camino und die Häuser zwischen der Rua As Rodas und der Rua Valle-Inclan gehören. Die über dem Hang aufragenden Granitfassaden des Museums stellen genau die empfindliche Balance zwischen Vergangenheit und Zukunft her, die der Architekt anstrebte.

Siza selbst sagt: »Die Fassaden des Museums wirken monumental, weil sie fast keine Fenster besitzen. Aufgrund der fehlenden Details strahlen sie eine Kraft aus, die der der Kirche oder des Klosters nahekommt. Im Inneren bietet das Museum dem Besucher keine eindeutige Wegführung, sondern eher eine Reihe von Alternativen. Eines unserer Probleme bei diesem Projekt bestand darin, daß es zu Anfang weder eine Sammlung noch einen Museumsdirektor gab. Unsere einzige Chance bestand im Aufbau eines flexiblen Systems, das verschiedene Nutzungsmöglichkeiten erlaubte.«[1] Siza verwandte große Mühe darauf, die benötigten technischen Systeme (Sicherheit, Belüftung und Licht) mit Hilfe einer abgehängten Decke zu kaschieren. Dadurch gelang es ihm auch, sichtbare Deckenstrahler zu vermeiden und die von ihm angestrebte Atmosphäre der »Reinheit« zu erzeugen.

Die angeschlagenen Wirtschaftssysteme in Frankreich und Deutschland sind verantwortlich für ein immer langsameres Tempo beim Bau neuer Museen. England dagegen, das Frankreich seit langem um den kulturellen Interventionismus Mitterrands beneidete, plant heute eine Reihe künstlerisch orientierter Bauprojekte – nicht zuletzt mit dem Geld der sehr erfolgreichen National Lottery. Auf diese Weise sollen eine Reihe interessanter Projekte finanziert werden, wie beispielsweise Norman Fosters ehrgeizige Erweiterungspläne des British Museum.

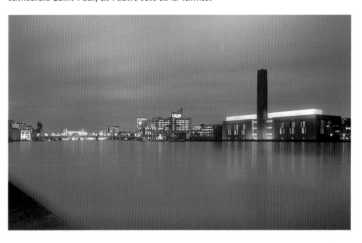

d'art contemporain fait partie intégrante d'une zone plus étendue qui englobe le couvent de San Roque, la porte Camino et les maisons situées entre la rue As Rodas et la rue Valle-Inclan. Surgissant de la colline, les façades en granit du musée parviennent à réaliser l'équilibre délicat entre passé et présent recherché par l'architecte. Selon lui, «les façades du musée sont monumentales parce qu'elles sont presque dépourvues de fenêtres. L'absence de détails leur donne une force comparable à celle de l'église ou du couvent. A l'intérieur, le musée ne suggère pas d'itinéraire au visiteur, mais plutôt une série d'alternatives. L'un des problèmes rencontrés au cours de ce projet a été que, au début, il n'y avait ni collection ni conservateur. La seule solution était donc de créer un système flexible, qui permette différents types d'utilisation».[1] Dans le contexte de la construction d'un musée d'art contemporain, il est intéressant de noter que Siza a fait un effort considérable pour masquer les dispositifs techniques indispensables (sécurité, ventilation et éclairage) à l'intérieur d'un plafond suspendu. Il a évité l'utilisation de spots visibles et créé ainsi l'ambiance de «pureté» recherchée.

Les problèmes économiques actuels de la France et de l'Allemagne ont eu pour conséquence un ralentissement du rythme de construction de nouveaux musées. L'Angleterre, longtemps envieuse de l'interventionnisme culturel de la France sous la présidence de Mitterrand, est aujourd'hui sur le point de créer une nouvelle série de projets à vocation culturelle. En effet, des fonds de la très fructueuse Loterie nationale sont désormais thésaurisés dans ce but. Selon toute probabilité, des fonds seront ainsi collectés pour la réalisation d'un certain nombre de projets intéressants, dont l'ambitieux plan d'agrandissement du British Museum vers la rotonde désormais libérée par le départ de la British Library. Ce dernier projet a été confié à Norman Foster.

En avril 1994, les architectes suisses Herzog & de Meuron ont été sélectionnés pour concevoir la nouvelle Tate Gallery of Modern Art à Londres, sur le site de l'ancienne centrale électrique du Bankside, face à la cathédrale Saint-Paul, de l'autre côté de la Tamise. Destiné à offrir au moins 12 000 m² de surface d'exposition, ce nouvel édifice sera en partie financé par le Fonds

*Herzog & de Meuron, proposed Tate Gallery
of Modern Art, London, 1994. Interior view.*

*Herzog & de Meuron, Entwurf der Tate Gallery
of Modern Art, London, 1994. Innenansicht.*

*Herzog & de Meuron, projet pour la Tate Gallery
of Modern Art, Londres 1994. Vue intérieure.*

on the Lottery. On October 30, 1995, it was announced by the Millennium Commission that a grant of no less than £50 million had been awarded to the Tate for the Bankside rehabilitation. Located near the new Globe Theater, it is hoped that the Tate Gallery of Modern Art will permit the regeneration of an entire new quarter of London. It is estimated that the project, whose total cost will be £106 million "will create 650 jobs locally and 2,400 throughout London, generating approximately £50 million in additional economic activity each year in an area with very high levels of unemployment." Aside from any esthetic considerations related to the architectural plan, this description, contained in a Tate Gallery press release demonstrates the great attention given to the economic impact of any publicly funded cultural project. Costs and benefits are much more carefully studied now than in the past, and architects are bound to take this into consideration. Herzog & de Meuron were chosen over a stellar field of competitors, including David Chipperfield, Tadao Ando, Renzo Piano, Rafael Moneo and Rem Koolhaas, proving if need be the continued attraction of the well-known names of architecture for such important museum designs. Although the final scheme will emerge only after much work between the architects and the curators, it is clear that the new Tate Gallery of Modern Art will be an ode to strict simplicity, centered around a stripped down 150 meter long turbine hall. It is interesting to note that Jacques Herzog has declared, "I support the idea of the architect as artist, but I think that to apply the image of art to architecture is the worst thing you can do. Contemporary architecture tends to behave like an advertising copywriter; it exploits the field of art, taking advantage of art in order to renew its own image without reflecting its conceptual foundations – and everybody gets tired of applied images. To escape being trapped in the world of Post-Modern graphics, the architect can also over-react by finding himself converted into a pure pragmatist." The radical simplicity of Herzog & de Meuron, proof of a renewed interest in modernity in contemporary architecture, is thus their own argument for the status of the architect, not as "advertising copywriter" but as Artist, with a capital A.

Im April 1994 erhielten die Schweizer Architekten Herzog & de Meuron den Auftrag zum Entwurf der neuen Tate Gallery of Modern Art, die in Londons verlassener Bankside Power Station, gegenüber der St. Paul's Cathedral auf dem anderen Themseufer, entstehen soll. Die mindestens 12000 m² großen Ausstellungsräume des neuen Projektes werden teilweise aus Mitteln des englischen Millennium Fund finanziert, der von der National Lottery abhängig ist. Am 30. Oktober 1995 gab die Millennium Commission bekannt, daß der Tate Gallery für die Sanierung der Bankside ein Zuschuß von nicht weniger als 50 Millionen Pfund gewährt würde. Man hofft, die in der Nähe des neuen Globe Theater gelegene Tate Gallery of Modern Art werde ihren Teil zur Wiederbelebung eines völlig neu sanierten Londoner Stadtviertels beitragen. Gleichzeitig wird davon ausgegangen, daß dieses insgesamt 106 Millionen Pfund teure Projekt »etwa 650 Arbeitsplätze vor Ort und 2400 in ganz London schaffen wird sowie für ein jährliches Wirtschaftsaufkommen von durchschnittlich 50 Millionen Pfund sorgt, und dies in einem Gebiet mit sehr hoher Arbeitslosenrate«. Diese, einer Presseveröffentlichung der Tate Gallery entnommene Beschreibung zeigt, daß neben allen ästhetischen Erwägungen, die mit solchen architektonischen Plänen verbunden sind, die wirtschaftlichen Auswirkungen bei der Realisierung öffentlich geförderter Kulturprojekte eine immer größere Rolle spielen. Auch von den Architekten verlangt man, die Kosten-Nutzen-Rechnung in ihre Planungen einzubeziehen. Herzog & de Meuron setzten sich gegen hochkarätige Konkurrenz durch, darunter David Chipperfield, Tadao Ando, Renzo Piano, Rafael Moneo und Rem Koolhaas, was für die anhaltende Anziehungskraft bedeutender Museumsaufträge bei den berühmten Namen der Architekturszene spricht. Obwohl der endgültige Plan erst nach langen Beratungen zwischen den Architekten und dem Kuratorium feststehen dürfte, ist dennoch klar, daß es sich bei der neuen Tate Gallery of Modern Art um eine Ode an die strenge Schlichtheit handeln wird, die rund um eine demontierte, 150 Meter lange Turbinenhalle entsteht. Jacques Herzog erklärte dazu: »Ich unterstütze die Vorstellung vom Architekten als Künstler, bin aber der Ansicht, daß man

pour le Millénaire de la Grande-Bretagne, qui est alimenté par la Loterie. Le 30 octobre 1995, la Commission du Millénaire a annoncé l'attribution d'au moins 50 millions de livres à la Tate pour son projet de réhabilitation du Bankside. Située près du nouveau Globe Theatre, la Tate Gallery of Modern Art permettra de revitaliser et de dynamiser tout un nouveau quartier de Londres. D'après les estimations, ce projet, dont le coût total devrait s'élever à 106 millions de livres, «créera 650 emplois locaux et 2400 pour la ville de Londres, générant chaque année environ 50 millions de livres sous la forme d'activités économiques annexes dans une zone où le taux de chômage est très élevé». En dehors de toute considération esthétique, cette description, qui figure dans un communiqué de presse publié par la Tate Gallery, montre le très grand intérêt accordé à l'impact économique de tout projet culturel financé par des fonds publics. Les comptes sont étudiés de beaucoup plus près aujourd'hui que par le passé, et les architectes doivent en tenir compte. Herzog & de Meuron ont été choisis parmi de nombreux concurrents, dont David Chipperfield, Tadao Ando, Renzo Piano, Rafael Moneo et Rem Koolhaas, ce qui prouve, si besoin était, que les projets de musées de cette envergure continuent d'attirer les plus grands noms de l'architecture. Le plan final sera le fruit d'une longue collaboration entre les architectes et les conservateurs, mais il est déjà clair que la nouvelle Tate Gallery for Modern Art conjuguera sobriété et simplicité et s'articulera autour de l'ancienne salle des turbines, longue de 150 mètres et désormais vidée de ses turbines. Il est intéressant de relever ces propos de Jacques Herzog: «Je défends l'idée que l'architecte est un artiste, mais je pense qu'appliquer la notion d'art à l'architecture est la pire des choses à faire. L'architecture contemporaine a tendance à se comporter comme un rédacteur publicitaire: elle exploite le terrain de l'art, s'en inspire pour renouveler sa propre image sans tenir compte de ses fondements conceptuels. finalement, tout le monde se lasse des images prêtes à l'emploi. Pour échapper au piège de l'art graphique postmoderne, l'architecte peut aussi réagir de façon excessive et devenir un pur pragmatiste.» La simplicité radicale de Herzog & de Meuron est le signe

The Berlin Conundrum

For sheer size, no architectural project in the world rivals with the reconstruction of Berlin. In the Mitte area alone, historic heart of the city and of the former East Berlin, the Berlin Senate has counted no fewer than 900 planned construction projects. In 1995 the public construction budget was evaluated at 30 billion Deutsche marks and 16 million tons of earth were moved despite the fact that the largest projects – the new Chancellery, the future central railway station on the Lehrter Bahnhof site (von Gerkan, Marg und Partner, architects), and the triple Tiergarten Tunnel – have hardly begun.[2] With an economic growth rate running below 1% in 1995, Berlin is calling on some of the best known architects in the world to help shape its new role as capital of the reunified Germany. Thus, Jean Nouvel, Arata Isozaki, Aldo Rossi, Harry Cobb, Philip Johnson, Norman Foster, Renzo Piano, O.M. Ungers, Josef Paul Kleihues, Helmut Jahn, David Childs of SOM, Hans Kollhoff and others will leave their mark on the city. But this prodigious building project has struggled to find a real consensus about goals and styles of architecture. Rather than seeking to break new ground, the city's powerful director of building and housing, Hans Stimmann is in favor of what is called "critical reconstruction," which means the design of relatively modest buildings clad in stone or brick rather than glass and steel. It is no accident, apparently, that foreign architects like Zaha Hadid, Rem Koolhaas or Coop Himmelblau are not being called on to build in the new Berlin. As Vittorio Lampugnani, ex-director of the Deutsches Architekturmuseum in Frankfurt and organizer of the earlier IBA housing project with Josef Paul Kleihues, declared in the magazine *Der Spiegel*, "Architecture must reflect the social desire for uniformity, not in the sense of a new kind of neutrality, but as a matter of principle. Principle means 'unification' and 'generality'. [...] It is thus necessary to restore the heavily damaged architectural tissue of the city, which does not require innovation at any price, but rather the repair of what exists."[3] Reacting violently against this point of view in the magazine *Arch+*, the American architect Daniel Libeskind, who has long been working on an extension

nichts Schlimmeres tun kann, als das Image der Kunst auf die Architektur zu übertragen. Die zeitgenössische Architektur neigt dazu, sich wie ein Werbetexter zu verhalten; sie beutet die Kunst aus und benutzt sie, um das eigene Image zu erneuern, ohne dabei an die eigenen konzeptuellen Grundlagen zu denken – und wir alle werden dieses aufgesetzten Images müde. Um dieser Welt der postmodernen Bilder zu entfliehen, kann der Architekt auch überreagieren, bis er sich – zum reinen Pragmatiker verwandelt – wiederfindet.« Die radikale Schlichtheit von Herzog & de Meuron, Beweis eines wiedererwachten Interesses an der Moderne in der zeitgenössischen Architektur, ist daher ihr bestes Argument für den Status des Architekten – nicht als »Werbetexter«, sondern als anerkannter Künstler.

Das Berlin-Rätsel

Was den Umfang angeht, kann sich kein anderes architektonisches Vorhaben weltweit mit dem Wiederaufbau Berlins messen. Allein in Berlin Mitte, dem historischen Zentrum der Stadt, hat der Berliner Senat 900 geplante Bauprojekte gezählt. Der gesamte Bauetat betrug 1995 geschätzte 30 Billionen DM, und 16 Millionen Tonnen Erde wurden bereits bewegt, obwohl die größten Projekte – das neue Bundeskanzleramt, der zukünftige Hauptbahnhof auf dem Gelände des Lehrter Bahnhofs (von Gerkan, Marg und Partner) sowie der dreiadrige Tiergarten-Tunnel – noch nicht sehr weit gediehen sind.[2] Trotz einer Wachstumsrate von unter 1% wandte sich Berlin an einige der berühmtesten Architekten der Welt, die seiner neuen Rolle als Hauptstadt des wiedervereinigten Deutschland Form verleihen sollen. Aus diesem Grunde werden Jean Nouvel, Arata Isozaki, Aldo Rossi, Harry Cobb, Philip Johnson, Norman Foster, Renzo Piano, O.M. Ungers, Josef Paul Kleihues, Helmut Jahn, David Childs von SOM sowie Hans Kollhoff der Stadt ihren Stempel aufdrücken. Aber anstatt mit diesem großartigen Bauvorhaben architektonisches Neuland zu erschließen, befürwortet Hans Stimmann, der mächtige Senatsbaudirektor der Stadt, die sogenannte »Kritische Rekonstruktion«, die den Entwurf relativ anspruchsloser stein- oder ziegelverkleideter Bauwerke »moder-

d'un regain d'intérêt de l'architecture contemporaine pour la
modernité. Elle illustre leur conception du statut de l'architecte,
considéré non pas comme un «rédacteur publicitaire», mais
comme un artiste, avec un grand A.

L'énigme berlinoise

Ne serait-ce que par son ampleur, la reconstruction de Berlin est
le projet architectural le plus important du monde. Dans le Mitte
seul (le cœur historique de la ville mais aussi de l'ancien Berlin
Est), le sénat berlinois a dénombré au moins 900 projets. En
1995, le budget de la construction publique était évalué à 30 bil-
lions de marks. 16 millions de tonnes de terre ont été déplacés.
Pourtant, les projets les plus importants viennent à peine de
commencer: la nouvelle chancellerie, la future gare centrale, qui
occupera l'emplacement de la Lehrter Bahnhof (agence von
Gerkan, Marg et Associés), ainsi que le triple tunnel de
Tiergarten.[2] Berlin, dont le taux de croissance économique n'a
même pas atteint 1% en 1995, fait appel à quelques-uns des
architectes les plus renommés du monde pour définir son allure
de nouvelle capitale de l'Allemagne réunifiée. Ainsi Jean Nouvel,
Arata Isozaki, Aldo Rossi, Harry Cobb, Philip Johnson, Norman
Foster, Renzo Piano, O.M. Ungers, Josef Paul Kleihues, Helmut
Jahn, David Childs of SOM, Hans Kollhoff et d'autres marque-
ront-ils la ville de leur empreinte. Toutefois, cette prodigieuse
entreprise de reconstruction a eu des difficultés à créer un véritable consensus quant aux objectifs et aux styles architecturaux.
Hans Stimmann, le très influent directeur de la construction et
du logement berlinois, ne cherche pas à innover, mais plutôt à
encourager la «reconstruction critique», c'est-à-dire la création
de bâtiments relativement modestes, habillés de pierre ou de
brique, de préférence au verre et à l'acier. Apparemment, ce n'est
pas un hasard si on n'a pas fait appel à des architectes étrangers
comme Zaha Hadid, Rem Koolhaas ou Coop Himmelblau.
Comme Vittorio Lampugnani, l'ex-directeur du Deutsches
Architekturmuseum de Francfort et co-organisateur, avec Josef
Paul Kleihues, du projet de logements IBA, l'a déclaré au magazine «Der Spiegel»: «L'architecture doit refléter le désir social

Christo & Jeanne-Claude, "Wrapped Reichstag",
Berlin, Germany, 1971–95.
© Christo 1995
Photo: Wolfgang Volz

Christo & Jeanne-Claude, »Verhüllter Reichstag«,
Berlin, Deutschland, 1971–95.
© Christo 1995
Photo: Wolfgang Volz

Christo & Jeanne-Claude, «Le Reichstag Empaqueté»,
Berlin, Allemagne, 1971–95.
© Christo 1995
Photo: Wolfgang Volz

to the Berlin Museum said, "The project for Berlin, capital of Germany shows just how the machinery of a bureaucratic administration can slowly transform a development which could have been inspiring and dynamic into a terrifyingly mediocre result. The decisions which were made there all ran against what would have been a unique occasion in the 20th century: to make Berlin an energetic city, turned toward the future [...] Good architecture is not the parody of history, but its articulation. The point is not to erase history but to confront it."[4]

Libeskind's dramatic zigzag design for the Jewish Museum in Berlin may not renew the history of contemporary architecture as much as he would claim, but it does seem diametrically opposed to the largely uninspiring designs of Hans Kollhoff and Helga Timmermann for the Alexanderplatz, or O.M. Ungers' block-like Friedrichstadt Passagen structure. Since Kleihues, Ungers and Kollhoff seem to have been in agreement with Hans Stimmann, their view has prevailed in the make-up of the new Berlin. Even the temerity of Frank O. Gehry seems to have been reigned in by the city's restrictions. The 17-story tower he is to build in the Pariserplatz will have a straightforward facade with a limestone

nen« Konstruktionen aus Glas und Stahl vorzieht. Daher ist es kein Zufall, daß Architekten wie Zaha Hadid, Rem Koolhaas oder Coop Himmelblau nicht um ihre Mitarbeit gebeten wurden. Vittorio Lampugnani, ehemaliger Direktor des Deutschen Architekturmuseums in Frankfurt und zusammen mit Josef Paul Kleihues Organisator der Internationalen Bauausstellung (IBA), erklärte dem »Spiegel«: »Das Bauen muß den sozialen Anspruch spiegeln, der ihm zugrunde liegt: es muß gleichförmiger werden. Nicht im Sinne einer Abflachung, sondern einer neuen, unerschrockenen Konvention. Konvention meint ›Vereinbarung‹ und ›Herkommen‹. [...] Dafür muß zunächst einmal die bestehende Bausubstanz, die in weiten Teilen nicht mehr benutzbar ist, restauriert werden: was keinerlei naseweise Neuinterpretation verlangt, sondern lediglich Reparatur.«[3] Dieser Auffassung widersprach der amerikanische Architekt Daniel Libeskind, der seit langem an einer Erweiterung des Berlin Museums baut, im Magazin »Arch+« auf das heftigste: »Bei der Planung Berlins als Hauptstadt Deutschlands sieht man, wie im langsam malenden Räderwerk einer von Bürokraten beherrschten Verwaltung zu deprimierender Mittelmäßigkeit stumpfgeschmirgelt wird, was eine beherzte und inspirierte Entwicklung hätte sein können. Ihre Entscheidungen sind weit von einer in 100 Jahren einmaligen Gelegenheit entfernt: Die Chance, eine sprühende, in die Zukunft greifende Stadt zu schaffen. [...] Bedeutsame Architektur zu schaffen heißt nicht, Geschichte zu parodieren, sondern sie zu artikulieren, heißt nicht, Geschichte auszulöschen, sondern sich mit ihr auseinanderzusetzen.«[4] Libeskinds dramatischer Zickzack-Entwurf für das Jüdische Museum in Berlin stellt zwar nicht unbedingt einen Neubeginn in der Geschichte der zeitgenössischen Architektur dar, steht aber dennoch im krassen Gegensatz zu den größtenteils uninspirierten Entwürfen von Hans Kollhoff und Helga Timmermann für den Alexanderplatz oder O.M. Ungers blockartiger Friedrichstadt-Passage. Aber da Kleihues, Ungers und Kollhoff im Einvernehmen mit Stimmann zu stehen scheinen, konnte sich ihr Konzept für den Bau des neuen Berlin durchsetzen. Selbst die Kühnheit eines Frank O. Gehry hat sich

d'uniformité, pas dans le sens d'une nouvelle neutralité, mais comme un point de principe. Par principe, j'entends ‹unification› et ‹généralité›. [...] Ainsi, il est nécessaire de restaurer le tissu architectural de la ville, qui a subi de gros dommages et nécessite non pas des innovations à tout prix, mais la remise en état de ce qui existe.»[3] L'architecte américain Daniel Libeskind, qui travaille depuis longtemps sur l'extension du Musée de Berlin, a violemment réagi à ce point de vue dans le magazine «Arch+»: «Le projet pour Berlin, capitale de l'Allemagne, démontre tout à fait comment la machine bureaucratique peut lentement transformer ce qui aurait pu être une création exaltante et dynamique en un résultat terriblement médiocre. Toutes les décisions qui ont été prises allaient à l'encontre de ce qui aurait constitué une occasion unique au XXe siècle: faire de Berlin une ville énergique et tournée vers l'avenir [...] La bonne architecture n'est pas une parodie de l'histoire, mais son expression. Le but n'est pas d'effacer l'histoire, mais de la regarder en face.»[4] Même si les zigzags spectaculaires créés par Libeskind pour le Musée juif de Berlin ont peu de chances de révolutionner l'histoire de l'architecture contemporaine autant que leur auteur le prétend, ils sont à l'évidence diamétralement opposés aux réalisations décevantes de Hans Kollhoff et Helga Timmermann pour la célèbre Alexanderplatz, ou au bâtiment à l'allure de bloc conçu par O.M. Ungers pour le Friedrichstadt Passagen. Depuis que Kleihues, Ungers et Kollhoff semblent partager les idées de Hans Stimmann, leur vision domine la mise en place du nouveau Berlin. Les restrictions imposées par la ville semblent même avoir réfréné les élans téméraires de Frank O. Gehry. La tour de 17 étages qu'il doit construire sur la Pariserplatz affichera une façade toute simple, habillée de calcaire, qui rappellera la Porte de Brandebourg voisine.

Dans une ville où l'innovation architecturale n'a peut-être pas joué un rôle très important, quelques événements remarquables ont eu un caractère franchement éphémère. Ce phénomène pourrait être perçu comme contraire à la «continuité» historiquement ambiguë recherchée par Hans Stimmann. Par exemple, Christo & Jeanne-Claude sont célèbres pour leurs

cladding much like that of the nearby Brandenburg Gate. In a city where architectural innovation may not have been granted a substantial role, some of the most outstanding events have had a decidedly ephemeral nature, which might be seen as opposing the historically ambiguous "continuity" sought by Hans Stimmann. Christo & Jeanne-Claude, for example, are well known for their wrapping of various objects, including the Pont Neuf in Paris. But their most difficult and most architectural work was certainly the 1995 "Wrapped Reichstag," in Berlin. Obviously, the complex history of this building and its central place in the German psyche, together with the decision that it would once again become the seat of the Bundestag, made the Christos' project all the more controversial. A shroud, even a silver one may have brought forth memories both within Germany and abroad about the past and the future of Berlin. Although temporary, this skin of cloth illustrates the potential for meaningful symbiosis between art and architecture. After a somewhat controversial competition, Norman Foster was of course selected to rebuild the Reichstag, but repeated intervention from within the parliament led him to adopt a domed design which seems much less original than the enormous canopy which he had originally conceived.

Along the former Berlin Wall corridor, one of the most prestigious construction sites is of course the Leipziger/Potsdamer Platz, an area of approximately 8 hectares where shopping centers, offices, and residential blocks are being designed by Piano, Moneo, Rogers, Isozaki, Kollhoff and others. A number of the partners in this vast enterprise, the Senatsverwaltung für Bau- und Wohnungswesen (Senate Administration for Civil Engineering), Deutsche Bahn AG, Debis, Sony/Tishman/Speyer and ABB/R. Ernst decided in 1994 to build a temporary information pavilion in the midst of the construction area. A competition, won by the Frankfurt firm, Schneider + Schumacher resulted in the construction of the Info Box, a 2,230 m² facility, in the record time of three months, between June and October 1995. Set up on 7 meter high concrete filled steel posts, the bright red Info Box is covered with 2,500 x 500 mm enameled steel plates. Inside,

anscheinend von den Beschränkungen der Stadt zähmen lassen: Der 17 Stockwerke hohe Turm, den er am Pariser Platz bauen soll, wird eine einfache Fassade mit einer Kalksteinverblendung erhalten, die stark an das nahe gelegene Brandenburger Tor erinnert.

In einer Stadt, in der der architektonischen Innovation keine tragende Rolle gewährt wird, zeichneten sich einige außergewöhnliche Ereignisse durch ihren entschieden vergänglichen Charakter aus, der im Gegensatz zu der historisch zweifelhaften »Kontinuität« eines Hans Stimmann zu stehen scheint. Christo & Jeanne-Claude beispielsweise sind berühmt für das Verhüllen verschiedenster Objekte; aber ihre schwierigste und zugleich architektonischste Arbeit war der »Verhüllte Reichstag« 1995. Die komplexe Geschichte des Bauwerks, sein zentraler Platz im deutschen Bewußtsein sowie die Entscheidung, dieses Gebäude erneut zum Sitz des Bundestags zu machen, ließ das Vorhaben der beiden Künstler natürlich besonders kontrovers erscheinen. Ein Leichentuch, selbst ein silbernes, würde in Deutschland wie auch im Ausland einen Schatten auf die Vergangenheit und die Zukunft Berlins werfen. Obwohl vergänglich, ließ diese Haut aus Stoff etwas vom Potential der bedeutungsvollen Symbiose von Kunst und Architektur erahnen. Nach einem umstrittenen Wettbewerb erhielt natürlich Norman Foster den Auftrag zum Umbau des Reichstags, aber wiederholte Interventionen des Parlaments führten dazu, daß Foster letztendlich eine Kuppel entwarf, obwohl sein ursprüngliches Projekt – ein enormer Baldachin – wesentlich origineller gewesen wäre.

Der im früheren Bereich der Berliner Mauer gelegene Leipziger/Potsdamer Platz gehört zu den prestigeträchtigsten Bauplätzen der Stadt. Auf diesem etwa 8 Hektar großen Areal entstehen Einkaufszentren, Büros und Wohnbauten, die von Architekten wie Piano, Moneo, Rogers, Isozaki, Kollhoff und anderen entworfen wurden. Einige Partner bei diesem riesigen Unternehmen – die Senatsverwaltung für Bau- und Wohnungswesen, Deutsche Bahn AG, Debis, Sony/Tishman/Speyer und ABB/R. Ernst – entschieden sich 1994 für den Bau eines Informationspavillons mitten auf dem Baugelände. Der Wettbewerb,

*Future view of the Alexanderplatz as designed
by Hans Kollhoff and Helga Timmermann.
Oil painting.*

*Zukünftige Ansicht des von Hans Kollhoff und
Helga Timmermann entworfenen Alexanderplatzes.
Ölgemälde.*

*Vue de la future Alexanderplatz, conçue par
Hans Kollhoff et Helga Timmermann.
Peinture à l'huile.*

empaquetages, notamment celui du Pont-Neuf à Paris.
Néanmoins, leur travail le plus difficile et le plus architectural fut
certainement «Le Reichstag Empaqueté», Berlin, en 1995. De
toute évidence, l'histoire compliquée de ce bâtiment et la place
prépondérante qu'il occupe dans l'inconscient allemand, parallè-
lement à la décision que le bâtiment redeviendrait le siège du
Bundestag, a soulevé d'autant plus de polémiques autour du
projet de Christo. Tant en Allemagne qu'à l'étranger, un linceul,
même en argent, aurait pu évoquer des souvenirs à propos du
passé et du futur de Berlin. En dépit de son caractère temporaire, cette «peau» symbolise la possibilité d'une symbiose
constructive entre l'art et l'architecture. Après un concours
quelque peu contesté, c'est bien sûr Norman Foster qui a été
sélectionné pour reconstruire le Reichstag, mais des interven-
tions répétées des parlementaires eux-mêmes l'ont amené à
adopter un projet incluant un dôme, qui semble beaucoup
moins original que l'énorme verrière prévue à l'origine.

Le long du couloir correspondant à l'ancien mur de Berlin, la
Leipziger/Potsdamer Platz représente l'un des emplacements
les plus prestigieux. Cette zone d'environ 8 hectares sera occupée par des centres commerciaux, des bureaux et des immeubles résidentiels conçus par Piano, Moneo, Rogers, Isozaki,
Kollhoff et d'autres. En 1994, le Senatsverwaltung für Bau- und

white gypsum boards, service conduits exposed at the ceiling level and black linoleum floor on timber boards affirm the "rough" look which the architects assumed to meet the tight schedule and 10 million mark budget. A 1,000 m² exhibition area, souvenir shop, and spaces for the sponsors sit beneath a roof-top café which offers a view on the Reichstag and former area of the wall. Because of its bright color, its unusual morphology, its intentionally ephemeral design and its situation in the midst of a vast work site, the Info Box could be considered quite the opposite of the continuity sought by Berlin's city planners. That might just be why it is an interesting building as well.

The Return of the Finns
Finnish architects have of course had a substantial impact on the evolution of modern forms. The most obvious name in this respect is that of Alvar Aalto (1898–1976) whose buildings demonstrated the breadth and strength of which modernism was capable. "Alvar Aalto's work has meant the most to me of all the work of the Modern masters," has written Robert Venturi. In his seminal 1966 essay, *Complexity and Contradiction in Architecture*, Venturi praised Aalto for his rejection of "simplification – that is, simplicity through reduction – in order to promote complexity with the whole." The Saarinens, Eliel (1873–1950) and his son Eero (1910–61) are amongst the best known Finnish architects, perhaps because of their work in the United States. Structures like Eero Saarinen's TWA Terminal at Idlewild (now Kennedy) Airport in New York (1956–62) figure rightfully in every text book on modern architecture. Other important Finnish figures ventured less beyond their own borders and are consequently little known outside of architectural circles. Such is the case of Aulis Blomstedt (1906–79) who sought out the fundamental laws of architecture, basing his theories on the dimensions of the human body and on musical harmony. Reima Pietilä (1923–93), another important figure of recent Finnish architecture, like Aalto worked on a number of church projects, of which the best known is the Kaleva Church (Tampere, Finland, 1959–66) which integrates a plan based on

den die Frankfurter Firma Schneider + Schumacher für sich entschied, führte zum Bau der sogenannten Info Box, eines 2230 m²
großen Gebäudes, das in der Rekordzeit von drei Monaten
errichtet wurde (Juni – November 1995). Die leuchtend rote Info
Box steht auf 7 Meter hohen, betongefüllten Stahlpfeilern und ist
mit 2500 x 500 mm großen, emaillierten Stahlplatten verkleidet.
Im Inneren verstärken weiße Gipskartonplatten, freiliegende
Versorgungsrohre unter der Decke und ein schwarzer Linoleum-
boden über hölzernen Dielen den »groben« Eindruck, mit
dem die Architekten dem engen Zeitplan und dem Budget von
10 Millionen Mark begegneten. Unterhalb eines Dachcafés, das
einen Ausblick auf den Reichstag und das frühere Gelände der
Mauer bietet, befinden sich eine 1000 m² große Ausstellungsfläche, ein Souvenirladen sowie Räumlichkeiten für die Spon-
soren. Aufgrund ihrer leuchtenden Farbe, der ungewöhnlichen
Form, des bewußt kurzlebigen Entwurfs und ihrer Lage inmitten
des riesigen Baugeländes erscheint die Info Box wie das genaue
Gegenteil der »Kontinuität«, die Berlins Stadtplaner anstreben.
Dies könnte ein Grund dafür sein, warum das Gebäude so inter-
essant wirkt.

Die Rückkehr der Finnen

Finnische Architekten haben bei der Entwicklung moderner
Formen eine bedeutende Rolle gespielt. Der in dieser Hinsicht
bekannteste Name ist Alvar Aalto (1898–76), dessen Bauwerke
die ganze Bandbreite und Kraft der Moderne demonstrierten.
Robert Venturi schrieb: »Von allen Meistern der Moderne besitzen Alvar Aaltos Arbeiten die größte Bedeutung für mich.«
In seinem 1966 erschienenen Essay »Komplexität und Wider-
spruch in der Architektur« rühmte Robert Venturi Aalto für seine
Ablehnung der »Vereinfachung – das heißt, Einfachheit durch
Reduzierung –, um die Komplexität im Ganzen zu unterstüt-
zen«. Auch die Saarinens, Eliel (1873–1950) und sein Sohn Eero
(1910–61), gehören zu den bekanntesten Architekten Finnlands,
nicht zuletzt aufgrund ihrer Arbeiten in den USA. Bauwerke wie
Eero Saarinens TWA Terminal auf dem Idlewild (heute Kennedy)
Airport in New York (1956–62) finden sich zu Recht in jedem

Wohnungswesen (Administration sénatoriale du génie civil), la
Deutsche Bahn AG, Debis, Sony/Tishman/Speyer et ABB/R.
Ernst, tous partenaires dans cette vaste entreprise, ont décidé de
construire un centre d'information temporaire au milieu du
chantier. La société Schneider + Schumacher de Francfort a remporté le concours pour la construction de l'Info Box, un complexe de 2230 m² construit en un temps record de trois mois, de
juin à octobre 1995. Juché sur des poteaux de 7 mètres en acier
remplis de béton, le bâtiment rouge vif est recouvert de plaques
en acier émaillé de 2500 x 500 mm. A l'intérieur, les murs en placoplâtre blanc, les conduits apparents au niveau du plafond et
les sols en linoléum noir posé sur bois contribuent à donner cet
aspect «brut» que les architectes ont adopté pour respecter
les délais très brefs et ne pas dépasser le budget de 10 millions
de marks. Le bâtiment contient une salle d'exposition de
1000 m², une boutique de souvenirs et des espaces réservés aux
sponsors, tandis que le toit est occupé par un café donnant sur
le Reichstag et une partie de l'ancien Mur. Par sa couleur, sa
morphologie inhabituelle, sa conception volontairement éphémère et sa situation au milieu d'un vaste chantier, l'Info Box
pourrait être considéré comme à l'opposé de la continuité
recherchée par les urbanistes berlinois. C'est peut-être ce qui
le rend d'autant plus intéressant.

Le retour des Finlandais

Les architectes finlandais ont eu une influence considérable sur
l'évolution des formes modernes. Le premier d'entre eux est
Alvar Aalto (1898–1976). Ses réalisations témoignent du souffle
et de la force dont le modernisme était capable. «De tous les
maîtres modernes, c'est Alvar Aalto qui a le plus compté pour
moi», avoue Robert Venturi. Dans son essai déterminant,
«Complexité et contradiction en architecture» (1966), Venturi
félicite Aalto d'avoir rejeté la «simplification – c'est-à-dire la simplicité atteinte au moyen de la réduction – afin de promouvoir la
complexité du tout». Eliel Saarinen (1873–1950) et son fils Eero
(1910–61) comptent parmi les architectes finlandais les plus
connus, peut-être parce qu'ils ont travaillé aux Etats-Unis. C'est

the Christian fish symbol with a stunningly modern design. The dominance of Aalto contributed to the impression of a decline in Finnish architecture after he passed from the scene, but it would appear that new figures of international importance are again emerging from this northern stronghold of modernism. The most obvious evidence of this rise is the attribution of the prestigious 1995 Carlsberg Prize to Juha Leiviskä.

Born in 1936, Leiviskä is in many senses an heir to the strong modern tradition established in Finland by Aalto and Blomstedt. He shares with them a feeling that there should be a relation between architecture and music. As he has said, "I remember a nightmare in which I had to find a link between the ground floor plan of Aalto's Finlandia hall in Helsinki and the last movement of the Hammerklavier sonata, opus 106, by Beethoven, which contains the most difficult fugue that I know of."

"The siting, the basic solution of a building", continues Leiviskä, "is the melody line in which the system of protection and opening are defined. It is a whole. After the first notes, the others follow; the beginning contains the end. Being an architect is like composing for a symphony that began thousands of years ago, and which extends through time. The architectural work entails enriching it, adding on movements. Each building and each space has to be created in harmony with the grand overall drama."

"The process of movement in a musical work," according to the Finnish architect, "is of the same order as the progression of an observer through architectural space. A sonata by Mozart or a song by Schubert both express the idea of an itinerary within a space: between each movement, there are pauses, crescendos, diminuendos and modulations of all kinds."[5]

Leiviskä's Männistö Church and Parish Center (Kuopio, Finland, 1986–92), is a testimony to his mastery of light and form, and undoubtedly to the continuing validity of modernism. Leiviskä himself explains at least part of the reason that Finland continues to produce great modern architecture when he says, "We Finns never sought to break with our history, probably because our heritage is extremely modest, what with so many fires and the ravages of the war. Our history is all the more

Buch über moderne Architektur. Andere bedeutende finnische Architekten wagten sich weniger weit über die heimischen Grenzen hinaus und sind daher außerhalb der Architekturszene nur wenig bekannt. Dies gilt z.B. für Aulis Blomstedt (1906–79), der nach den Grundgesetzen der Architektur forschte und seine Theorien auf die Dimensionen des menschlichen Körpers und auf die Harmonielehre stützte. Reima Pietilä (1923–93) arbeitete wie Aalto an einer Reihe von Kirchenbauten; seine bekannteste Arbeit ist die Kaleva-Kirche (Tampere, Finnland, 1959–66), deren Entwurf einen Grundriß auf der Basis des christlichen Fischsymbols mit einem verblüffend modernen Design kombiniert.

Der 1936 geborene Juha Leiviskä, Gewinner des Carlsberg-Preises 1995, ist in vieler Hinsicht ein Erbe der starken modernen Tradition, die Aalto und Blomstedt in Finnland begründeten. Wie seine Vorgänger glaubt er an eine Beziehung zwischen Architektur und Musik. Leiviskä sagt: »Ich erinnere mich an einen Alptraum, in dem ich eine Verbindung finden sollte zwischen dem Grundriß von Aaltos Finlandia Hall in Helsinki und dem letzten Satz von Beethovens Sonate für Hammerklavier, Opus 106, die die schwierigste Fuge enthält, die ich kenne.«

»Die Anlage, der grundlegende Gedanke eines Gebäudes«, fährt Leiviskä fort, »entspricht einer Melodielinie, in der das System von Schutz und Öffnung definiert ist. Es handelt sich um ein Ganzes. Nach den ersten Noten folgen die anderen; der Anfang trägt das Ende in sich. Die Arbeit als Architekt gleicht dem Komponieren an einer Symphonie, die vor Jahrtausenden begann und im Laufe der Zeit ständig erweitert wird. Die architektonische Arbeit bedeutet deren Bereicherung, das Hinzufügen neuer Sätze. Jedes Bauwerk und jeder Raum muß in Harmonie mit der großen Gesamtkomposition erschaffen werden«. »Der Fortgang der Bewegung in einem musikalischen Werk«, sagt Leiviskä, »entspricht der Bewegung eines Beobachters durch den architektonischen Raum. Einer Mozart-Sonate oder einem Schubertlied liegt ebenfalls die Vorstellung einer Reise durch den Raum zugrunde: zwischen jedem Satz findet man Pausen, Crescendi, Diminuendi und Modulationen aller Art.«[5]

ainsi que le terminal TWA de Idlewild (aujourd'hui Kennedy)
Airport construit par Eero Saarinen à New York (1956–62) figure
à juste titre dans tous les livres sur l'architecture moderne.
D'autres architectes finlandais restent peu connus en dehors
des cercles professionnels parce qu'ils se sont moins aventurés
à l'étranger. C'est le cas de Aulis Blomstedt (1906–79), qui a
exploré les lois fondamentales de l'architecture, en fondant ses
théories sur les mensurations du corps humain et sur l'harmonie musicale. Comme Aalto, Reima Pietilä (1923–93), autre
figure marquante de l'architecture finlandaise, a travaillé sur un
certain nombre d'églises. La plus connue est celle de Kavela
(Tampere, Finlande, 1959–66), dont le plan étonnamment
moderne s'inspire du symbole chrétien du poisson. L'architecture finlandaise a semblé en déclin lorsque la personnalité domi-
nante de Aalto a disparu de la scène. Pourtant, il semblerait que
des personnalités de stature internationale émergent de nouveau de ce fief nordique du modernisme. La preuve en est l'attribution du prestigieux prix Carlsberg 1995 à Juha Leiviskä.

Né en 1936, Leiviskä est à plus d'un titre l'héritier d'une forte
tradition moderne établie par Aalto et Blomstedt. Il partage avec
eux le sentiment qu'il devrait exister un rapport entre architecture et musique. «Je me souviens d'un cauchemar où je devais
trouver un lien entre le plan du rez-de-chaussée du Finlandia
Hall d'Aalto à Helsinki et le dernier mouvement de la sonate
pour piano dite ‹Hammerklavier›, opus 106 de Beethoven, qui
contient la fugue la plus difficile que je connaisse», raconte
Leiviskä, qui poursuit: «Point de départ d'une construction,
l'emplacement est la ligne mélodique dans laquelle sont définis
les systèmes de protection et d'ouverture. C'est un tout. Les premières notes passées, les autres suivent; la fin est contenue
dans le commencement. L'architecte compose pour une symphonie commencée il y a des milliers d'années et se prolongeant
à travers les âges. Son travail consiste à l'enrichir, à y ajouter des
mouvements. Chaque édifice et chaque espace doit être créé en
harmonie avec la formidable mise en scène universelle.»

Selon Leiviskä, «dans une œuvre musicale, le mouvement est
du même ordre que celui d'un observateur avançant dans un

Heikkinen-Komonen, Embassy of Finland, Washington, D.C., 1989–94. Interior view.

Heikkinen-Komonen, Finnische Botschaft, Washington, D.C., 1989–94. Innenansicht.

Heikkinen-Komonen, Ambassade de Finlande à Washington, D.C., 1989–94. Vue intérieure.

important. Because of this, modernity did not constitute a break for us, but rather the assertion of an identity. In other countries, more often than not, architects hated preceding periods. The functionalists hated Art Nouveau. They needed virgin space. But this wasn't the case in Finland."

More modest than many internationally recognized architects, Leiviskä, beyond his close relation to Finland, seeks a deeper connection between the built form and the natural world. He says, "I believe in the permanency of the basic features of architecture, the so-called external values. I do not therefore believe that there has been anything in recent years which could revolutionize the basic tenets of architecture or its central task."

Mikko Heikkinen, born in 1949 in Helsinki, and Markku Komonen, born in the same city in 1945, created their firm in 1974. Komonen was the editor-in-chief of *Arkkitehti Magazine* from 1977 to 1980 and Director of the Exhibition Department of the Museum of Finnish Architecture from 1978 to 1986. Known for their Heureka Finnish Science Center completed in Helsinki in 1988, or the European film School in Denmark (1989–93), Heikkinen-Komonen have recently built the new Embassy of Finland in Washington, D.C. Despite being located on Massachusetts Avenue in the heart of Washington's embassy district, this 4,750 m² structure gives an impression of a close communion with nature. Indeed, there are more than 20 different species of trees on the site, some of them more than 30 meters tall, and the openings of the building, together with features like the bronze trellis for climbing plants on the street side enhance the relation of the Embassy to its green surroundings. The Embassy of Finland is certainly a sign to the outside world that this country continues to be a source of interesting architectural design.

New Dutch Talents

For a variety of reasons related to its geographic situation and its tradition as a base for art and trade, architectural talent seems to emerge from The Netherlands with great regularity. In recent years, the success of Rem Koolhaas has provided an example to the younger generation. One particularly interesting

Leiviskäs Männistö Kirche und Gemeindezentrum (Kuopio, 1986–92) zeugt ebenso von seinem meisterhaften Umgang mit Licht und Form wie von der fortdauernden Gültigkeit der Moderne. Leiviskä selbst erklärt, warum Finnland weiterhin große moderne Architektur hervorbringt: »Wir Finnen haben nie versucht, mit unserer Geschichte zu brechen. Dies liegt vielleicht daran, daß unser Erbe aufgrund der vielen Brände und Verwüstungen des Krieges so extrem bescheiden erscheint. Daher ist unsere Geschichte umso wichtiger. Aus diesem Grunde stellte die Moderne keinen Bruch für uns dar, sondern eher die Behauptung unserer Identität. In anderen Ländern haßten die Architekten häufig die vorhergehenden Stilperioden. Die Funktionalisten haßten Art Nouveau; sie benötigten jungfräulichen, unverbauten Raum. Dies war in Finnland nicht der Fall.«

Über seine enge Beziehung zu Finnland hinaus sucht Leiviskä nach einer tieferen Verbindung zwischen gebauter Form und Natur. Er sagt: »Ich glaube an die Beständigkeit der grundlegenden Merkmale der Architektur, an die sogenannten äußeren Werte. Daher kann ich nicht glauben, daß es in den letzten Jahren etwas gegeben hat, das die Grundsätze der Architektur oder ihre zentrale Aufgabe revolutionieren könnte.«

Mikko Heikkinen und Markku Komonen, 1949 bzw. 1945 in Helsinki geboren, gründeten ihre Firma 1974. Heikkinen-Komonen wurden bekannt durch ihr 1988 in Helsinki erbautes Finnisches Wissenschaftszentrum Heureka sowie den Bau der European Film School in Dänemark (1989–93); vor kurzem stellten sie die neue Finnische Botschaft in Washington, D.C. fertig. Trotz seiner Lage an der Massachusetts Avenue, mitten im Herzen des Washingtoner Diplomatenviertels, vermittelt dieses 4750 m² große Bauwerk den Eindruck einer engen Verbundenheit mit der Natur. Auf dem Gelände stehen mehr als 20 verschiedene Baumarten, die teilweise über 30 Meter hoch sind. Die Gebäudeöffnungen betonen ebenso wie das bronzene Spalier für Kletterpflanzen auf der Straßenseite die Beziehung des Bauwerks zur grünen Umgebung. Die neue Finnische Botschaft zeigt ihrer Umwelt, daß dieses Land nach wie vor eine Fülle interessanter architektonischer Entwürfe hervorbringt.

espace architectural. Une sonate de Mozart ou un lied de Schubert expriment l'idée d'un itinéraire dans l'espace: entre deux mouvements, il y a des pauses, des crescendo, des diminuendo et des modulations de toutes sortes».[5]

L'église et le centre paroissial de Männistö (Kuopio, Finlande, 1986–92) témoignent de la maîtrise de Leiviskä quant à la lumière et à la forme, mais aussi de la pérennité du modernisme. Leiviskä explique lui-même pourquoi son pays continue de produire de grandes œuvres d'architecture moderne: «Nous autres finlandais n'avons jamais cherché à rompre avec notre histoire, probablement parce que notre héritage est très modeste, à cause des nombreux incendies et des ravages causés par la guerre. Notre histoire est d'autant plus importante. C'est pourquoi, pour nous, la modernité n'a pas constitué une rupture, mais plutôt l'affirmation d'une identité. Dans d'autres pays, la plupart du temps, les architectes détestent les périodes précédentes. Les fonctionnalistes détestaient l'Art Nouveau. Ils avaient besoin d'espace vierge. Ce n'était pas le cas en Finlande.»

Plus modeste que beaucoup d'architectes mondialement connus, Leiviskä, au-delà de ses liens étroits avec la Finlande, cherche à créer un lien entre la forme construite et la nature. «En architecture, je crois en la permanence des caractéristiques essentielles, appelées valeurs externes, explique-t-il. Ces dernières années, je ne pense pas qu'il y ait eu quoi que ce soit de bouleversé quant aux principes essentiels ou au travail architectural.»

Mikko Heikkinen et Markku Komonen, nés à Helsinki respectivement en 1949 et en 1945, ont créé leur cabinet en 1974. Komonen a été rédacteur en chef de «Arkkitehti Magazine» de 1977 à 1980 et responsable des expositions au Musée de l'architecture finlandaise de 1978 à 1986. Heikkinen et Komonen sont connus pour leur Centre scientifique finlandais Heureka achevé en 1988 à Helsinki, ainsi que pour l'Ecole européenne du cinéma (Danemark, 1989–93). Ils viennent de construire la nouvelle ambassade de Finlande à Washington, D.C. Bien que situé sur Massachusetts Avenue, au cœur du quartier des ambassades, cet édifice de 4750 m² crée une impression de communion avec

member of this group is Ben van Berkel, born in Utrecht in 1957. Van Berkel, a 1987 graduate of the Architectural Association (AA) in London where Koolhaas taught, says, "I am from a different generation of architects than Rem Koolhaas and Zaha Hadid, and I am critical of that generation. I was taught by them at the AA, but I feel that they always tried too hard to develop theories. In their work, the theory became the image of the theory. If there is to be some form of architectural theory, we would apply it in a more tactile, more physical way, in the sense of rethinking typologies of spatial organization or the use of materials. The point is that we are not working with an emblem of a theory or with the representation of a manifesto. If you think of Bernard Tschumi, Rem Koolhaas and Peter Eisenman, their work was almost a kind of decorum of their own anti-architectural concepts."[6] Although he is mild-mannered, Ben van Berkel speaks with a quiet determination and in a surprising way, relegates his elders to an already distant past. Although most of his work to date has been on small scale projects located in Amersfoort near Amsterdam, he has taken the step to a much larger and more visible kind of project with the new Erasmus Bridge in Rotterdam. With its unusual single 139 meter high pylon, this bridge is the last north-south connection before the port of Rotterdam and the North Sea, and it sits just at the entrance to the central part of the city. When Ben van Berkel is asked about the apparent visual similarity of this bridge to Santiago Calatrava's 1992 Puente del Alamillo on the Guadalquivir River in Seville, he readily makes reference to the fact that he did work with Calatrava before creating his own firm, van Berkel & Bos in 1988, but he quickly sets the record straight. "There may be a kind of similarity between this bridge and Calatrava's bridge. The relation of the height to the length in Calatrava's case is 1 : 1. Here it is 1 : 2, which means that the length is very great in relation to the height of the pylon. This pylon had to have an incredible amount of force. The angle of the pylon permitted a reduction of its height. The quality of a bridge also depends on the thinness of the deck, and according to my engineers, this is one of the thinnest in the world for this length – it is only 2.10 meters."[7]

Neue niederländische Talente

Aus einer Reihe von Gründen, die eng mit der geographischen Lage und einer Tradition als Ausgangspunkt für Kunst und Handel zusammenhängen, scheinen die Niederlande mit großer Regelmäßigkeit immer neue architektonische Talente hervorzubringen. In den letzten Jahren diente vor allem Rem Koolhaas als leuchtendes Beispiel für die jüngere Generation. Ein besonders interessanter Vertreter dieser Gruppe ist der 1957 in Utrecht geborene Ben van Berkel. Van Berkel, der 1987 die Architectural Association (AA) in London abschloß, an der auch Koolhaas lehrte, erklärt: »Ich stamme aus einer anderen Architektengeneration als Rem Koolhaas oder Zaha Hadid, und ich stehe deren Generation kritisch gegenüber. Ich wurde von ihnen an der AA ausgebildet, aber ich glaube, daß sie immer zu sehr mit der Entwicklung von Theorien beschäftigt waren. In ihren Arbeiten wurde die Theorie zum Bild der Theorie. Wenn überhaupt eine Architekturtheorie existiert, würde ich sie auf eine greifbare, physische Art und Weise umsetzen, wobei die Typologien der räumlichen Organisation oder die Verwendung der Materialien neu überdacht werden müßten. Der Punkt ist, daß wir nicht mit dem Symbol einer Theorie oder der Verkörperung eines Manifestes arbeiten. Die Arbeiten von Bernard Tschumi, Rem Koolhaas oder Peter Eisenman wirken beinahe wie eine Art Dekorum ihrer eigenen, anti-architektonischen Konzepte.«[6] Obwohl es sich bei den meisten seiner bisherigen Arbeiten um kleinere Projekte handelt, die in Amersfoort, in der Nähe von Amsterdam, entstanden, hat van Berkel mit der neuen Rotterdamer Erasmusbrug den Schritt zu einem wesentlich größeren und auffälligeren Bauvorhaben gewagt. Mit ihrem ungewöhnlichen, 139 Meter hohen Pylon stellt diese Brücke die letzte Nord-Süd-Verbindung vor dem Rotterdamer Hafen und der Nordsee dar und liegt genau am Eingang zum inneren Stadtzentrum. Wenn man van Berkel auf die offensichtliche Ähnlichkeit seiner Brücke zu Santiago Calatravas 1992 entstandener Puente del Alamillo über den Guadalquivir in Sevilla anspricht, weist er bereitwillig darauf hin, daß er vor der Gründung seiner eigenen Firma van Berkel & Bos (1988) für Calatrava arbeitete, stellt aber

la nature. On y trouve une vingtaine d'espèces différentes d'arbres, dont certains atteignent plus de 30 mètres. Les ouvertures du bâtiment, alliées à des éléments tels qu'un treillage en bronze couvert de plantes grimpantes côté rue, renforcent l'harmonie entre le bâtiment et la végétation alentour. L'ambassade de Finlande signale clairement au reste du monde que ce pays demeure une source de création architecturale non négligeable.

Les nouveaux talents hollandais

Pour diverses raisons liées à la situation géographique des Pays-Bas et à leur rôle traditionnel de centre artistique et économique, il semble que des talents architecturaux y naissent très régulièrement. Ces dernières années, le succès de Rem Koolhaas a servi de modèle à la jeune génération. Un architecte se distingue plus particulièrement: Ben van Berkel, né à Utrecht en 1957 et diplômé en 1987 de l'Architectural Association (AA) à Londres, où enseignait Koolhaas. «J'appartiens à une génération d'architectes différente de celle de Rem Koolhaas et Zaha Hadid, et je porte sur leur époque un regard critique. J'ai suivi leurs cours à la AA, et je pense qu'ils ont toujours cherché à mettre au point une théorie. Dans leur travail, la théorie est devenue l'image de la théorie. S'il doit y avoir une quelconque forme de théorie architecturale, il faudrait l'appliquer d'une façon plus tactile, plus physique, en repensant les typologies de l'organisation spatiale et l'utilisation des matériaux. Le problème, c'est que nous ne travaillons pas avec une théorie emblématique ou avec la représentation d'un manifeste. Ainsi, les créations de Bernard Tschumi, Rem Koolhaas et Peter Eisenman étaient presque une sorte d'illustration systématique de leurs concepts anti-architecturaux.»[6] Malgré son caractère modéré, Ben van Berkel parle avec une calme détermination et, curieusement, relègue ses aînés dans un passé déjà lointain. Jusqu'ici, son travail se limitait à de petits chantiers à Amersfoort, près d'Amsterdam, mais il vient de passer à une dimension supérieure avec le nouveau pont Erasmus, à Rotterdam. Ce pont, dont l'originalité réside dans son unique pylône haut de 139 mètres, est la dernière liaison nord-sud avant le port de Rotterdam et la mer du Nord. Il se

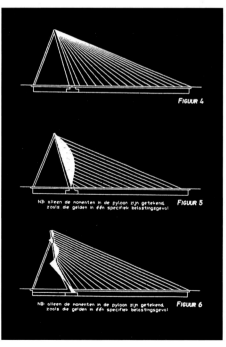

Ben van Berkel, Karbouw Office and Workshop, Amersfoort, The Netherlands, 1990–92. Side view showing the profiled aluminum cladding.

Ben van Berkel, Bürogebäude und Werkstatt der Firma Karbouw, Amersfoort, Niederlande, 1990–92. Seitenansicht der Profilaluminium-Verkleidung.

Ben van Berkel, Bureau et Atelier Karbouw, Amersfoort, Pays-Bas, 1990–92. Vue latérale montrant le revêtement en aluminium profilé.

Ben van Berkel's involvement with a bridge project, normally the province of engineers is in itself unusual, but his approach to other, more traditionally architectural designs also shows where he differs from his elders. Eschewing references to contemporary art, which seem to be quite fashionable with his generation of architects, he prefers to delve into the technical or scientific aspects of his profession, speaking of the "responsibility" of architects. He is particularly interested in the impact of computer assisted design on the kind of buildings which can now be produced. As he says, "I think for example that the way computers can give us information in several layers is very important. We can generate so many more different images than we could before. It has become possible to design with the computer now. It is a kind of hybridization which permits the architect to convert a sketch into a form which can be built. Maybe there is a kind of artistry in this. I am always afraid, however, that an architect who is too artistic becomes very academic. Architects can't really be only artists. We have more responsibility. Twenty thousand people will use the Erasmus Bridge every day. You have to think about these 'daily life' aspects of architecture, and the scientific part of it too."[8] "I like to believe that you can invent as an architect, like a scientist does", concludes Ben van Berkel. This is a message of optimism and a plea in favor of architectural originality coming from one of the most talented younger architects working in Europe today.

Another Dutch figure to be reckoned with is Erick van Egeraat. Born in 1956 in Amsterdam, he attended the Technical University of Delft's Department of Architecture, from which he graduated in 1984. A co-founder of Mecanoo Architects in 1983, he created

sofort klar: »Natürlich könnte man von einer gewissen Ähnlichkeit zwischen dieser Brücke und Calatravas Brücke sprechen. In Calatravas Fall beträgt das Verhältnis von Höhe zu Länge 1:1. Hier ist es 1:2, was bedeutet, daß die Länge im Verhältnis zur Höhe des Pylonen wesentlich größer ist. Dieser Pylon mußte ungeheuer kräftig ausfallen; sein Neigungswinkel erlaubte jedoch die Reduzierung seiner Höhe. Daneben hängt die Qualität einer Brücke auch von der Dünne der Brückentafel ab, und laut meinen Ingenieuren handelt es sich hier, im Verhältnis zu ihrer Länge, um eine der dünnsten Brücken der Welt – nur 2,10 Meter dick.«[7]

Ben van Berkels Arbeit an einem Brückenprojekt – normalerweise eine Domäne der Ingenieure – mag ungewöhnlich erscheinen, aber auch sein Umgang mit anderen, traditionelleren architektonischen Aufgaben zeigt, daß er sich von seinen Vorgängern unterscheidet. Er vermeidet Bezüge zur zeitgenössischen Kunst – ein bei den Architekten seiner Generation beliebter Trend – und sucht statt dessen die Auseinandersetzung mit den technischen und wissenschaftlichen Aspekten seines Berufs, wobei er von der »Verantwortung« der Architekten spricht. Van Berkel ist besonders an den Möglichkeiten des computergestützten Designs und dessen Auswirkungen auf neue Bauformen interessiert. »Für mich ist es sehr wichtig, daß ein Computer uns Informationen in verschiedenen Schnitten vermitteln kann. Dadurch sind wir in der Lage, sehr viel mehr unterschiedliche Bilder zu erzeugen als jemals zuvor. Heute ist es möglich, direkt am Computer zu entwerfen. Es findet eine Art Hybridisierung statt, die es dem Architekten erlaubt, eine Skizze in eine Form umzuwandeln, die gebaut werden kann. Vielleicht steckt darin eine Art künstlerischer Leistung. Ich habe allerdings immer Angst davor, daß ein zu künstlerischer Architekt sehr akademisch wird. Architekten können nicht nur Künstler sein. Wir tragen eine größere Verantwortung. Die Erasmusbrug wird jeden Tag von 20000 Menschen benutzt werden. Man darf diese ›alltäglichen‹ Aspekte von Architektur ebensowenig aus den Augen verlieren wie den wissenschaftlichen Teil dieser Arbeit.«[8] »Ich gebe mich gern der Illusion hin, daß man als Architekt ebenso wie ein

situe juste à l'entrée du centre de la ville. Interrogé sur la ressemblance entre ce pont et le Puente del Alamillo réalisé en 1992 par Santiago Calatrava sur le Guadalquivir, à Séville, l'architecte précise aussitôt qu'il a effectivement travaillé avec Calatrava avant d'ouvrir son propre cabinet, van Berkel & Bos, en 1988. Puis il s'empresse de préciser: «Il existe peut-être des ressemblances entre les deux ponts. Cependant, dans le cas du Puente del Alamillo, le rapport hauteur-longueur est de 1:1, alors qu'ici il est de 1:2. La longueur est donc énorme par rapport à la hauteur du pylône, qui devait avoir une force incroyable. L'angle du pylône a permis de réduire sa hauteur. La qualité d'un pont dépend aussi de la minceur du tablier et, d'après mon équipe d'ingénieurs, celui-ci est l'un des moins épais au monde (seulement 2,10 m) relativement à sa longueur.»[7]

Le fait que Ben van Berkel ait entrepris de réaliser un pont est inhabituel en soi, puisqu'il s'agit normalement d'un domaine réservé aux ingénieurs. Par ailleurs, son approche d'autres domaines de création architecturale plus traditionnels montre aussi en quoi il se distingue de ses aînés. Contrairement aux architectes de sa génération, van Berkel évite toute référence à l'art contemporain. Il préfère se plonger dans les aspects techniques et scientifiques de sa profession, et évoque la «responsabilité» de l'architecte. Il s'intéresse en particulier à la conception assistée par ordinateur et à son impact sur les bâtiments réalisés aujourd'hui. Ainsi explique-t-il: «Je pense que le fait que les ordinateurs peuvent nous fournir des renseignements sur plusieurs niveaux est très important. Nous pouvons créer infiniment plus d'images différentes qu'auparavant. Aujourd'hui, il est possible de concevoir un projet sur ordinateur. C'est une sorte d'hybridation qui permet à l'architecte de convertir un dessin en une forme qui peut être construite. Cette technique relève peut-être de l'art. Cependant, je redoute toujours qu'un architecte trop artiste ne devienne aussi très académique. L'architecte ne peut pas être seulement un artiste. Il a une autre responsabilité. 20000 personnes par jour vont emprunter le pont Erasmus. On est obligé de réfléchir à ces aspects «quotidiens» de l'architecture, mais aussi aux aspects

Erick van Egeraat associated architects in 1995. He recently completed the renovation of a building for the ING Group in Budapest, Hungary. Van Egeraat carefully restored this white 1882 Italianate building located on Andrassy ùt – the local equivalent of the Champs-Elysées. From street level, it seems that hardly anything has changed, but the two top floors added by the architect are dominated by the "whale", an organic blob that bursts through the glass roof onto the skyline of Budapest. Containing the boardroom, this extrusion is the focus of the project. It appears to float on a plane of glass that also functions as the roof. Its organic forms contrast with the exposed lift machinery. All the more significant in Budapest because the city has undergone a period of 50 years during which architectural innovation was all but excluded, this unusual combination of late 19th and late 20th century architecture is the fruit of the collaboration between the huge Internationale Nederlanden Groep NV (ING) represented by the Czech born Paul Koch now living in Holland and the architects. ING is the group which bought the Barings Bank after its financial fiascoes in March 1995. It is one of Europe's largest banking and insurance companies, with a 1994 net profit of $1.49 billion. An admirer of Jean Nouvel, Frank O. Gehry and Van Egeraat, ING's representative Paul Koch has commissioned them to work in Prague. Gehry's much publicized Rasin building in Prague, called "Fred and Ginger" or the "Dancing Building" and attacked by Prince Charles, is the result of work carried out by ING, again represented by Koch, the Prague-based Sarajevo born architect Vladimir Milunic and Gehry himself.

Clearly, in order for innovative architects to be given a chance to make the shape of the built environment evolve, it is necessary for them to have clients who are willing to take risks. This condition has unfortunately been met far too rarely at a time of rising economic and political conservatism. The NN/ING building deals with the problems of the renovation of an historic structure in an unusual way, and it is interesting to note that the American magazine *Architecture* wrote in its November 1995 editorial that "One has only to look at the glass mansard and cocoon designed by the Dutch architect [...] atop an Italianate

Wissenschaftler etwas erfinden kann«, erklärt Ben van Berkel – eine optimistisches Plädoyer für architektonische Originalität von einem der talentiertesten jungen Architekten Europas.

Ein weiterer aufstrebender niederländischer Architekt ist Erick van Egeraat. 1956 in Amsterdam geboren, besuchte er das Institut für Architektur an der Technischen Hochschule Delft, wo er 1984 sein Diplom erhielt. Nach seiner Tätigkeit als Mitbegründer von Mecanoo Architects (ab 1983) eröffnete er 1995 Erick van Egeraat associated architects. Vor kurzem beendete van Egeraat in Budapest die Renovierung eines Gebäudes für die Nationale Nederlanden and ING Group. Dieses weiße Neo-Renaissance-Gebäude, das 1882 an der Andrassy ùt – dem Budapester Gegenstück zur Champs-Elysées – entstand, wurde von van Egeraat sorgfältig restauriert. Vom Straßenniveau aus betrachtet, hat sich kaum etwas verändert, aber die beiden vom Architekten hinzugefügten obersten Geschosse werden vom »Wal« dominiert – einem organischen Gebilde, das durch das Glasdach in die Skyline Budapests ausbricht. Diese »Extrusion« (in der sich der Sitzungssaal des Vorstandes befindet) bildet den optischen Mittelpunkt des Gebäudes. Sie scheint auf einer Fläche aus Glas zu treiben, die zugleich als Dach des Gebäudes dient, und ihre organischen Formen stehen im Kontrast zu der freigelegten Technik des Lifts. Diese ungewöhnliche Kombination aus der Architektur des späten 19. und des ausgehenden 20. Jahrhunderts ist das Ergebnis einer Zusammenarbeit zwischen einem der größten europäischen Finanz- und Versicherungsunternehmen, dem Großkonzern Internationale Nederlanden Group NV (ING), repräsentiert von dem in der tschechischen Republik gebürtigen und heute in den Niederlanden lebenden Stadtplaner Paul Koch, und den Architekten. ING, repräsentiert durch Paul Koch, der ein Bewunderer von Jean Nouvel, Frank O. Gehry und van Egeraat ist, verhalf diesen zu Aufträgen in Prag. Gehrys Prager Rasin Gebäude, bekannt als »Fred und Ginger« oder »Tanzendes Gebäude«, und heftig von Prinz Charles attackiert, ist das Ergebnis einer Zusammenarbeit von ING – repräsentiert durch Koch – dem in Sarajevo gebürtigen, in Prag lebenden Architekten Vladimir Milunic sowie Gehry.

Erick van Egeraat, Nationale Nederlanden and ING
Bank, Budapest, Hungary, 1992–94. An interior view
showing the intersection of the old structure with the
added upper floors.

Erick van Egeraat, Nationale Nederlanden and ING
Bank, Budapest, Ungarn, 1992–94. Innenansicht,
auf der die Verbindung des alten Gebäudes mit den
zusätzlichen oberen Stockwerken zu sehen ist.

Erick van Egeraat, Nationale Nederlanden and ING
Bank, Budapest, Hongrie, 1992–94. Vue intérieure
montrant l'intersection de l'ancienne structure et des
étages supérieurs ajoutés.

scientifiques. J'aime à croire que l'architecte peut se montrer
inventif, comme un scientifique.»[8] Voilà, de la part d'un des
jeunes architectes européens les plus doués de sa génération,
un message d'optimisme et un plaidoyer en faveur de l'originalité architecturale. Erick van Egeraat est également une personnalité néerlandaise avec laquelle il faut compter. Né à Amsterdam
en 1956, il a obtenu son diplôme de l'université technique de
Delft en 1984. Cofondateur de l'agence Mecanoo en 1983, il a
créé en 1995 Erick van Egeraat et Associés. Il vient d'achever la
rénovation de la ING Group à Budapest. Il a soigneusement restauré ce bâtiment blanc de style italien datant de 1882 et situé
sur Andrassy ùt, l'équivalent des Champs-Elysées. Même si,
depuis la rue, il semble que presque rien n'ait changé, les deux
derniers étages rajoutés par l'architecte sont surmontés d'une
«baleine», forme floue intégrée à l'édifice et qui surgit à travers
la verrière, au-dessus des toits de la capitale hongroise. Cette
excroissance, qui abrite les bureaux de la direction, constitue le
point central du projet. Elle semble flotter sur le toit de verre, et
ses formes intégrées contrastent avec la machinerie apparente
de l'ascenseur. Ce mélange inhabituel de styles architecturaux
(fin XIXe et fin XXe siècle) prend d'autant plus d'importance à
Budapest que la ville n'a connu presque aucune innovation
depuis 50 ans. C'est le fruit de la collaboration entre le gigan-
tesque Internationale Nederlanden Groep NV (ING), représenté
par Paul Koch, promoteur d'origine tchèque installé en Hollande,
et les architectes. C'est ING, qui a racheté la Barings Bank après
son naufrage, en mars 1995. Avec un bénéfice net de 1,49 billion
de dollars, elle se classe parmi les plus importantes sociétés de
banque et d'assurance européennes. ING, représenté par Paul
Koch, qui admire Jean Nouvel, Frank O. Gehry et Van Egeraat, les
a aidés à obtenir des commandes à Prague. Surnommé «Fred
and Ginger» ou le «Dancing Building», le célèbre Rasin, construit
à Prague par Gehry et critiqué par le prince Charles, est le résultat
des efforts conjugués de ING, à nouveau représenté par Koch, de
Vladimir Milunic, architecte né à Sarajevo et installé à Prague, et
bien sûr Gehry lui-même.

Il est clair que, pour faire évoluer les formes architecturales de

Erick van Egeraat, Nationale Nederlanden and
ING Bank, Budapest, Hungary, 1992–94.
The "Whale" as it appears on the roof of the building.

Erick van Egeraat, Nationale Nederlanden and ING
Bank, Budapest, Ungarn, 1992–94. Der »Wal« auf
dem Dach des Gebäudes.

Erick van Egeraat, Nationale Nederlanden and
ING Bank, Budapest, Hongrie, 1992–94. La «Baleine»
telle qu'elle apparaît sur le toit du bâtiment.

block in Budapest to understand how experimental design ener-
gizes old buildings through contrast. It is difficult to imagine
preservationists in this country sanctioning such juxtapositions."[9] Van Egeraat's own description of this project gives
an idea of his creative process. "The Whale itself contains a boardroom and a coffee-corner. Her form is not modern. Her form is
also not revisionist. She is more reactionary than pragmatic,
more sensual than mechanistic [...] By the use of irregular curves,
it was possible to freely form the Whale with regards to a diversity
of internal spatial wishes. Her appearance therefore becomes
powerful but not overbearing. External factors, such as her spatial
counterform and the desire for southerly light to penetrate deep
in to the staircase, inspired an image of a modern lantern and it
was at this point that her definitive form was finally decided."

"The project as a whole", concludes Erick van Egeraat, "is thus
a modest manifesto against the repressive effect of misplaced
and carping conservatism and in favor of reinterpretation using
contemporary means without automatically resorting to High-
Tech." It is above all an interesting solution to the problem of
adaptive reuse which is posed all over Europe. Rather than simply
gutting an old building and keeping only its facades, as has been
common practice in recent years, Van Egeraat looks toward a
more symbiotic relationship with the past – a way forward which
integrates a rapport with history that is more than skin-deep.

Um innovativen Architekten die Möglichkeit zu geben, die Form der bebauten Umgebung weiterzuentwickeln, benötigt man Auftraggeber, die Interesse an diesen Tendenzen haben. Leider wurde diese Bedingung in einer Zeit des immer stärkeren politischen und wirtschaftlichen Konservatismus nur zu selten erfüllt. Das Budapester Nationale Nederlanden and ING-Gebäude setzt sich auf ungewöhnliche Weise mit dem Problem der Renovierung eines historischen Bauwerks auseinander. Interessanterweise schrieb das amerikanische Magazin »Architecture« in seiner Ausgabe vom November 1995: »Man braucht nur einen Blick auf die Glasmansarde und den Kokon zu werfen, den der niederländische Architekt [...] auf einen Häuserblock im Stil der Neo-Renaissance in Budapest setzte, um zu verstehen, wie experimentelles Design alten Gebäuden durch Kontraste neues Leben einhaucht. Es ist schwer vorstellbar, daß die Denkmalschützer in diesem Land ein derartiges Nebeneinander begrüßen würden.«[9]

Van Egeraats eigene Beschreibung des Projekts vermittelt eine Vorstellung seines kreativen Prozesses. »Der Wal enthält einen Sitzungssaal und eine Kaffeetheke. Seine Form ist nicht modern; seine Form ist auch nicht revisionistisch. Er ist eher reaktionär als pragmatisch, eher sinnlich als mechanistisch [...] Durch die Verwendung unregelmäßiger Kurven war es möglich, den Wal völlig frei zu formen und dabei eine Vielzahl interner räumlicher Wünsche zu berücksichtigen. Daher wirkt sein Erscheinungsbild kraftvoll, aber nicht anmaßend. Externe Faktoren wie seine räumliche Gegenform oder der Wunsch, das Licht von Süden möglichst weit in das Treppenhaus eindringen zu lassen, ließen mich an eine moderne Laterne denken, und an diesem Punkt habe ich mich für seine endgültige Form entschieden.«

»Das Projekt als Ganzes«, so van Egeraat weiter, »ist also eine maßvolle Grundsatzerklärung gegen die repressiven Auswirkungen eines unangebrachten, krittelnden Konservatismus und für eine Neuinterpretation mit Hilfe zeitgenössischer Mittel ohne automatischen Rückgriff auf ›High-Tech‹.« Vor allem handelt es sich um eine interessante Lösung des Problems der anpassungsfähigen Wiederverwendung, welches in ganz Europa

notre environnement, les architectes innovateurs ont besoin de clients prêts à prendre des risques. Malheureusement, à une époque où le conservatisme économique et politique va croissant, cette condition est trop rarement remplie. Le bâtiment de ING répond de façon originale aux problèmes posés par la rénovation d'un édifice historique. D'ailleurs, il est intéressant de relever ces propos dans l'éditorial du magazine américain «Architecture», en novembre 1995: «Il suffit de regarder la verrière mansardée, véritable cocon conçu par l'agence néerlandais [...], au sommet d'un immeuble à l'italienne de Budapest, pour comprendre comment des réalisations expérimentales peuvent revitaliser de vieux bâtiments en créant un contraste. On voit mal comment les défenseurs du patrimoine architectural de ce pays pourraient sanctionner de telles juxtapositions.»[9]

La description que fait Van Egeraat de son projet donne une idée de sa démarche créative: «La Baleine contient la salle du conseil d'administration et un coin-café. Sa forme n'est ni moderne, ni révisionniste. Elle est plus réactionnaire que pragmatique, plus sensuelle que mécaniste [...] L'utilisation de courbes irrégulières a permis de donner une forme à la Baleine en tenant compte de la diversité des souhaits concernant l'organisation spatiale intérieure. Dans son aspect, elle devient ainsi puissante sans être dominatrice. Des facteurs extérieurs tels que sa contreforme spatiale et le désir d'éclairer le plus profondément possible l'escalier par la lumière venant du sud, ont fait surgir la notion de lanterne moderne. C'est ainsi que sa forme s'est finalement imposée.»

Erick van Egeraat conclut: «Ainsi, l'ensemble du projet est un modeste manifeste contre l'effet répressif d'un conservatisme déplacé et malveillant et en faveur de la ré-interprétation par l'utilisation de moyens contemporains, sans pour autant faire automatiquement appel au high-tech.» Avant tout, il s'agit d'une solution intéressante au problème de la réutilisation adaptive qui se pose dans toute l'Europe. Au lieu de détruire un vieux bâtiment en ne conservant que sa façade, comme cela a souvent été le cas ces dernières années, Egeraat cherche à nouer une

Paris Streamline

The Grands Travaux, François Mitterrand's large urban projects, launched the careers of a number of French architects who are now internationally known, including Jean Nouvel and Christian de Portzamparc. Other firms of considerable talent have also emerged in recent years, such as Architecture Studio, which co-authored the Institut du Monde Arabe in Paris (completed in 1987) with Nouvel, and is currently building the massive new European Parliament in Strasbourg. Their Lycée Jules Verne, in Cergy-Le-Haut, France was completed in 1993. This 16,000 m² facility for 1,350 pupils was built for a construction cost of 108 million French francs. Although the architects cite the influence of the aerodynamic forms of the French TGV high-speed trains in the design of this high school, it resembles a space craft as much as anything else and thus fully justifies the name which it carries, that of France's greatest science fiction author. The philosophy of Architecture Studio, a collaborative venture created in 1973 which currently has six principal members, as they express it, certainly integrates a capacity to derive inspiration from the name of Jules Verne. "Slowly," they write, "in some respects too slowly because the dictatorship of rationalism lasted much longer in architecture than did that of abstraction vis-à-vis the figurative arts, architecture is returning to the expression of meaning. Architecture is returning to the use of decoration and nourishing its rapport with history. It is learning once again to intervene in a harmonious way in an existing environment, or even to create new environments, with a more balanced relationship with technology. Above all," they conclude, "architecture is once again learning to tell stories." The source of the "story" they tell in Cergy-Le-Haut near Paris is of course the fantasy world of Jules Verne, but it is also that of a new community which remains a kind of no-man's-land between "high voltage wires, and unbuilt lots, where this work in gray and blue challenges the upturned earth of a city under construction."[10]

Another decidedly aerodynamic or space-craft like form is that of the L'Oréal Factory, in Aulnay-sous-Bois, which is also near Paris, by Valode & Pistre. This 30,000 m² manufacturing and

immer wieder auftaucht. Anstatt einfach ein altes Gebäude zu entkernen und nur die Fassaden zu erhalten, sucht van Egeraat nach einer symbiotischen Verbindung mit der Vergangenheit – ein Schritt nach vorn, der eine Beziehung zur Geschichte herstellt, die mehr als nur oberflächlich ausfällt.

Paris Streamline

Die Grands Travaux, François Mitterrands große urbane Bauprojekte, waren der Karrierebeginn für eine Reihe französischer Architekten von inzwischen internationalem Ruf, wie Jean Nouvel und Christian de Portzamparc. In den letzten Jahren sind auch einige andere Architekten von bemerkenswertem Talent bekannt geworden. Dazu zählt die Gruppe Architecture Studio, die zusammen mit Nouvel das Institut du Monde Arabe in Paris entwarf (1987 fertiggestellt) und zur Zeit das gewaltige neue Europäische Parlament in Straßburg baut. Ihr Lycée Jules Verne im französischen Cergy-Le-Haut wurde 1993 fertiggestellt. Dieser 16 000 m² große Komplex für 1350 Schüler wurde mit einem Budget von 108 Millionen Francs realisiert. Obwohl die Architekten bei ihrem Entwurf die aerodynamischen Formen des französischen Hochgeschwindigkeitszuges TGV vor Augen hatten, erinnert das Gebäude ebenso stark an ein Raumschiff und rechtfertigt daher seinen Namen, den des größten französischen Science fiction-Autors. Die Philosophie des Architecture Studio schließt mit Sicherheit die Fähigkeit ein, sich von dem Namen Jules Verne inspirieren zu lassen. »Langsam«, so schreiben sie, »in mancher Hinsicht zu langsam – da die Diktatur des Rationalismus in der Architektur wesentlich länger währte als die der Abstraktion gegenüber der Bildenden Kunst – kehrt die Architektur zum Ausdruck der Bedeutung zurück. Die Architektur wendet sich wieder der Verwendung von Ornamenten zu und knüpft ihr Band zur Geschichte. Wieder einmal lernt sie, auf harmonische Weise in eine bestehende Umgebung einzugreifen, oder sogar eine neue Umgebung zu schaffen, mit einem ausgewogeneren Verhältnis zur Technologie. Vor allem lernt die Architektur wieder einmal, Geschichten zu erzählen.« Die »Geschichte«, die sie in Cergy-Le-Haut, in der Nähe von Paris, erzählt, basiert natürlich

relation plus symbiotique avec le passé, à intégrer un rapport
avec l'histoire qui soit davantage qu'un simple rapport superficiel.

Paris remodelé

Les Grands Travaux est le nom donné au grand projet urbain de
François Mitterrand qui a lancé un certain nombre d'architectes
français aujourd'hui connus dans le monde entier, parmi lesquels Jean Nouvel et Christian de Portzamparc. D'autres cabi-
nets talentueux se sont également distingués ces dernières
années. C'est le cas d'Architecture Studio – coauteur avec Jean
Nouvel de l'Institut du monde arabe, achevé à Paris en 1987 –,
qui travaille actuellement sur l'énorme projet du Parlement européen à Strasbourg. Leur lycée Jules-Verne à Cergy-le-Haut a été
achevé en 1993. Cet édifice de 16000 m² destiné à accueillir 1350
élèves a coûté 108 millions de francs. Les architectes disent
s'être inspirés des formes aérodynamiques du TGV (Train à grande vitesse), mais le lycée ressemble surtout à un vaisseau spatial
digne du très grand auteur français de science-fiction dont il
porte le nom. Née en 1973, Architecture Studio est une entreprise collective qui compte six collaborateurs. Leur philosophie leur
permet de toute évidence, et selon leurs propres termes, de
s'inspirer de Jules Verne. «Lentement, écrivent-ils, à certains
égards trop lentement, car le rationalisme a régné sur l'architecture beaucoup plus longtemps que l'abstraction dans le domaine des arts figuratifs, l'architecture revient au sens. Elle revient à
la décoration et nourrit sa relation privilégiée avec l'histoire. Elle
apprend de nouveau à intervenir de façon harmonieuse sur un
environnement donné, et même à créer de nouveaux environne-
ments qui entretiennent un rapport plus équilibré avec la technologie.» «Avant tout, concluent-ils, l'architecture apprend de
nouveau à raconter des histoires.» L'«histoire» qu'ils racontent
à Cergy-le-Haut, près de Paris, est inspirée du monde mer-
veilleux de Jules Verne, mais aussi d'une nouvelle commune,
une sorte de no man's land au milieu «de lignes à haute tension
et de terrains non construits, où cet édifice habillé de gris et de
bleu défie la terre retournée d'une ville en construction».[10]
    Conçue par Valode & Pistre, l'usine de L'Oréal à Aulnay-sous-

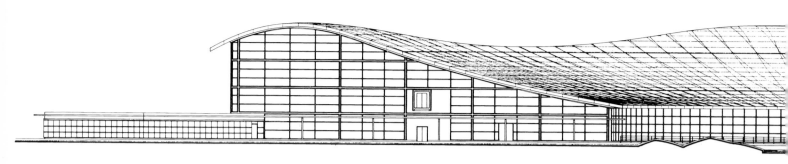

administrative complex is most notably marked by its enormous curved roof inspired by the image of a three-petaled flower floating above the ground. Made of an aluminum/polyethylene "sandwich" the roof elements, measuring 60 x 130 meters, are suspended without columns by a tubular space frame superstructure designed by the late engineer Peter Rice. The apparent and real lightness of the roof structure made it possible to bring far more light into the factory areas than is usually the case. Because of new production techniques, dividing the usual assembly line process of this cosmetics manufacturer into smaller units, the architects were able to propose this spectacular tripartite structure disposed around a central garden and artificial lake, rather than adhering to the more traditional rectilinear architecture of factories. The unusual curving complexity of the roof elements was made possible not only by computer assisted design but by a laser guided checking system for the placement of the 20,000 panels.

Combining an innovative structural solution with a renewed concept of factory layout, this project concludes this survey as well as any other. The L'Oréal factory shows that technology, new materials and a willingness on the part of clients and architects to experiment, have created the conditions for a true renewal of architecture.

New Images for Institutions

Institutions, particularly large ones, do not often have the reputation of seeking out architectural innovation when they plan new facilities. Three recent examples in France, which may bear some relationship to the architectural ambitions of François Mitterrand go very much in the opposite direction. Calling on talented architects, the Catholic Church in Evry, the European Court of Human Rights in Strasbourg and Mitterrand's own Bibliothèque nationale de France in Paris all show the advantages, and some of the limitations of applying the solutions of advanced design to institutions.

Mario Botta's Cathedral in Evry (1992–95) faces the problem of giving a center to a new city, created without any real sense

Valode & Pistre, L'Oréal Factory, Aulnay-sous-Bois, France, 1988–91. **Above:** *Drawing showing the roof structure.* **Below:** *Interior view.*

Valode & Pistre, L'Oréal-Werke, Aulnay-sous-Bois, Frankreich, 1988–91. **Oben:** *Zeichnung der Dachkonstruktion.* **Unten:** *Innenansicht.*

Valode & Pistre, Usine L'Oréal, Aulnay-sous-Bois, France, 1988–91. **Ci-dessus:** *Dessin montrant le toit de la structure.* **Ci-dessous:** *Vue intérieure.*

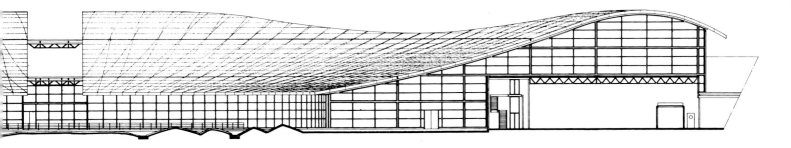

auf der Phantasiewelt des Jules Verne, aber es handelt sich ebenso um die Geschichte einer neuen Gemeinde in einem Niemandsland zwischen »Hochspannungsleitungen und brachliegenden Grundstücken, wo dieses Werk in Grau und Blau gegen die aufgeworfene Erde einer Stadt im Bau antritt«.[10]

Auch bei den L'Oréal-Werken, die die Architekten Valode & Pistre in Aulnay-sous-Bois, ebenfalls in der Nähe von Paris, erbauten, kann man fraglos von einer aerodynamischen, raumschiffähnlichen Form sprechen.

Das auffälligste Kennzeichen dieses 30 000 m² großen Produktions- und Verwaltungskomplexes ist seine enorme, geschwungene Dachkonstruktion, die einer dreiblättrigen, über dem Boden schwebenden Blüte nachempfunden wurde. Die aus einem Aluminium/Polyäthylen-Verbund hergestellten Dachelemente von 60 x 130 Metern wurden ohne Stützpfeiler an einem räumlichen Tragwerk aus Röhren aufgehängt, das der verstorbene Ingenieur Peter Rice entwarf.

Die Durchlässigkeit dieser Dachkonstruktion erlaubt es, daß wesentlich mehr Licht in die Fabrikationsbereiche einfallen kann als dies bisher der Fall war. Dank neuer Herstellungsverfahren, die die bisherige Fließbandfertigung des Kosmetikherstellers in kleinere Einheiten unterteilen, waren die Architekten in der Lage, auf die traditionelle, geradlinige Fabrikarchitektur zu verzichten und ihre aufsehenerregende, dreigeteilte Konstruktion rund um einen zentralen Garten und einen künstlichen See anzuordnen.

Der ungewöhnliche, komplizierte Schwung der Dachelemente wurde nicht nur durch computerunterstütztes Design ermöglicht, sondern auch mit Hilfe eines lasergesteuerten Prüfsystems, das die Justierung der 20 000 Platten übernahm. Mit ihrer Kombination einer innovativen strukturalen Lösung und einem neuartigen Fabrikdesign beweisen die L'Oréal-Werke, daß Technologie, neue Materialien und die Bereitschaft zum Experiment seitens der Auftraggeber und Architekten die Bedingungen für eine wahre Erneuerung der Architektur schaffen können.

Bois (près de Paris) évoque elle aussi la forme aérodynamique d'un vaisseau spatial. Cet espace de 30 000 m² renfermant chaînes de fabrication et services administratifs se singularise par son énorme toit, dont la forme arrondie rappelle celle d'une fleur à trois pétales flottant au-dessus du sol. Il est composé d'éléments de 60 x 130 mètres faits d'un «sandwich» aluminium/polyéthylène et maintenus sans la moindre colonne, grâce à une charpente tubulaire conçue par Peter Rice, ingénieur aujourd'hui disparu. La légèreté de ce toit permet de laisser pénétrer beaucoup plus de lumière que dans la plupart des usines. La mise au point de nouvelles techniques de production permettant de diviser la chaîne traditionnelle en unités plus petites, les architectes ont pu proposer cette spectaculaire structure tripartite centrée sur un jardin et un lac artificiel, délaissant ainsi l'architecture industrielle rectiligne, plus traditionnelle. La courbe singulièrement complexe du toit a pu être réalisée grâce à la conception assistée par ordinateur, mais aussi en faisant appel à un système de vérification par rayon laser qui a permis de placer les 20 000 panneaux. Ce projet, qui propose une structure originale en même temps qu'un nouveau concept d'usine, mérite tout à fait de conclure ce chapitre. L'usine L'Oréal apporte la preuve que la technologie, alliée à de nouveaux matériaux et à une volonté chez les clients et les architectes de tenter des expériences, peut créer les conditions d'un véritable renouvellement de l'architecture.

Les institutions changent d'image

Les institutions, en particulier les grandes, ont rarement la réputation de chercher à innover d'un point de vue architectural lors de la construction de nouvelles installations. Récemment pourtant, trois exemples français peut-être liés aux ambitions architecturales de François Mitterrand sont venus contredire cette tendance. En faisant appel à des architectes de talent, l'Eglise catholique (à Evry), la Cour européenne des droits de l'homme (Strasbourg) et la Bibliothèque nationale de France (Paris) ont montré les avantages mais aussi les limites de la création de pointe appliquée aux institutions.

La cathédrale d'Evry (1992–95) conçue par Mario Botta est

of urban design. Located just to the south of Paris, Evry is a rather ugly "ville nouvelle". Calling on the truncated cylindrical form that he seems to favor, Botta erected this 4,800 m² church with a reinforced concrete structure and brick cladding on both the exterior and interior. The apparently unusual form of the Cathedral, a 38.5 meter circular plan, in fact makes reference to Byzantine churches and in this respect looks back to the origins of Christianity. An unusual triangular metal frame carries the roof structure, admitting generous amounts of daylight, making the interior very agreeable if not obviously spiritual. Criticized as a costly venture which the church could ill afford, this Cathedral, the first built in France for more than a century in fact, proclaims the living faith shared by parishioners in this modern context. With the square in front of it, the Evry Cathedral gives some sense of a center to this ville nouvelle which is otherwise devoid of architectural inspiration. As he was in the case of his recent San Francisco Museum of Modern Art, Botta was criticized here for a somewhat heavy-handed approach.

After the art museum, the library may be one of the most potent symbols of cultural achievement and intellectual prowess. Although London has long been working on the new British Library, the most spectacular and largest library project anywhere in the world is most probably the last of the Grands Travaux of François Mitterrand. The so-called Bibliothèque nationale de France, is located in the 13th arrondissement of Paris in a zone formerly occupied essentially by the rail lines leading to the Austerlitz train station. With its 450 kilometers of bookshelves and 4,000 seats in the lecture rooms this 360,000 m² building stands out if only because of its size. The concept of four 100 meter high towers placed like "open books" around a central sunken garden was vigorously attacked by a number of eminent specialists not only because of the obvious difficulty in retrieving books placed in towers, but also because of the danger to the volumes exposed to light and heat in structures which were originally intended to be highly transparent. The project was modified to reduce the height of the towers, bet-

Neues Image für alte Institutionen

Viele, insbesondere große Institutionen stehen nicht gerade im Ruf, bei der Planung neuer Einrichtungen in die Grenzbereiche architektonischer Innovation vorstoßen zu wollen. Allerdings weisen drei aktuelle Beispiele in Frankreich, die eine gewisse Verwandtschaft mit den architektonischen Ambitionen François Mitterrands aufweisen, genau in die entgegengesetzte Richtung.

Dank der Arbeit talentierter Architekten zeigen die Kathedrale von Evry, der Europäische Gerichtshof für Menschenrechte in Straßburg und die von Mitterrand in Auftrag gegebene Bibliothèque nationale de France in Paris die Vorzüge, aber auch einige Grenzen der Anwendbarkeit moderner Entwurfsmethoden.

Mario Bottas Cathédrale d'Evry (1992–95) sieht sich dem Problem gegenüber, das Zentrum einer neuen Stadt sein zu müssen, die ohne jedes städtebauliche Fingerspitzengefühl entworfen wurde. Evry, am Südrand von Paris gelegen, ist eine relativ häßliche »ville nouvelle«. Unter Berufung auf die von ihm bevorzugte, stumpfe zylindrische Form errichtete Botta die 4800 m² große Kirche als Stahlbetonkonstruktion und versah sowohl das Innere als auch das Äußere mit einer Ziegelverblendung. Die auf den ersten Blick ungewöhnliche Form der Kathedrale – ein kreisförmiger Entwurf von 38,5 Meter Durchmesser – nimmt in Wahrheit den Grundriß byzantinischer Kirchen wieder auf und greift damit auf die Ursprünge des Christentums zurück. Die von einem ungewöhnlichen dreieckigen Metallrahmen getragene Dachkonstruktion läßt den Raum von Tageslicht durchfluten, wodurch das Innere der Kathedrale sehr angenehm, wenn nicht sogar spirituell wirkt. Kritisiert als kostspieliges Unterfangen, das sich die Kirche nur schlecht leisten könne, kündet die erste seit über 100 Jahren in Frankreich erbaute Kathedrale von einem lebendigen Glauben, der in diesem modernen Rahmen von den Gemeindemitgliedern geteilt wird. Zusammen mit ihrem Vorplatz erzeugt die Cathédrale d'Evry den Eindruck eines Stadtzentrums in dieser »ville nouvelle«, die ansonsten bar jeder architektonischen Inspiration zu sein scheint.

Mario Botta, Evry Cathedral, Evry, France, 1992–95.

Mario Botta, Cathédrale d'Evry, Evry, Frankreich, 1992–95.

Mario Botta, Cathédrale d'Evry, Evry, France, 1992–95.

censée donner un centre à cette ville nouvelle dépourvue de tout urbanisme cohérent. Située dans la banlieue sud de Paris, Evry est une ville moderne plutôt laide. Faisant appel à la forme d'un cylindre tronqué qu'il semble affectionner, Botta a fait ériger cette église de 4800 m² en béton armé recouvert de brique, à l'intérieur comme à l'extérieur. A priori inhabituel, le plan circulaire de 38,5 mètres fait référence aux églises byzantines et, par là même, aux origines de la chrétienté. Le toit, supporté par une surprenante charpente métallique triangulaire, laisse largement pénétrer la lumière du jour, ce qui rend l'intérieur très agréable sinon éminemment spirituel. Considérée par certains comme une aventure coûteuse que l'Eglise pouvait difficilement se permettre, cette cathédrale, la première construite en France depuis plus d'un siècle, proclame la foi vivante partagée par les paroissiens dans cet environnement moderne. La cathédrale d'Evry et son parvis font figure de centre pour cette «ville nouvelle» dépourvue par ailleurs de toute inspiration architecturale. De même que pour la récente construction du San Francisco Museum of Modern Art, on a reproché à Botta son approche quelque peu maladroite.

Juste après le musée, la bibliothèque est peut-être l'un des plus puissants symboles de la réussite culturelle et du talent intellectuel. Bien que Londres travaille depuis longtemps à la construction de la nouvelle British Library, le projet de bibliothèque le plus spectaculaire et le plus grand du monde est très probablement le dernier des Grands Travaux de François Mitterrand. La Bibliothèque nationale de France est située dans le XIIIe arrondissement de Paris, dans une zone précédemment occupée pour l'essentiel par les lignes de chemin de fer menant à la gare d'Austerlitz. Cet édifice de 360000 m² se singularise avant tout par sa taille. Il contiendra 450 kilomètres de rayonnages et 4000 places pour les lecteurs. Le concept, quatre tours de 100 mètres de haut disposées comme des «livres ouverts» autour d'un jardin central situé en contrebas, a été violemment critiqué par un certain nombre d'éminents spécialistes, non seulement en raison de la difficulté évidente pour accéder aux livres, mais aussi à cause du danger que représente pour les volumes

Dominique Perrault, Bibliothèque nationale de France, Paris, France, 1989–96.

Dominique Perrault, Bibliothèque nationale de France, Paris, Frankreich, 1989–96.

Dominique Perrault, Bibliothèque nationale de France, Paris, France 1989–96.

ter protect the volumes kept in them, and to increase the size of the stacks situated in the base of the complex. Despite a Modernist concept based in good part on the architect's admiration for Minimalist artists like Carl André and Richard Serra, the harsh aspects of the Bibliothèque are somewhat softened by the central garden, visible essentially from the reading rooms. By creating this sunken font of greenery, Dominique Perrault intended to make reference to the Garden of Eden, to the Original Sin and thus to the origin of the knowledge contained in the millions of volumes kept here. Perrault makes clear his own interest in art when he says, "The architecture of the library represents an attempt to create a work which is of its time.

Neben dem Kunstmuseum zählt die Bibliothek zu den mächtigsten Symbolen kultureller Errungenschaften und intellektueller Fähigkeiten. Obwohl in London seit langem an der neuen British Library gearbeitet wird, ist das aufsehenerregendste und größte Bibliotheksprojekt weltweit wahrscheinlich das letzte der Grands Travaux François Mitterrands. Die Bibliothèque nationale de France liegt im 13. Pariser Arrondissement, in einem Areal, das bis vor kurzem von den Gleisanlagen des Bahnhofs Gare d'Austerlitz beherrscht wurde. Dieses 360 000 m² große Bauwerk mit seinen 450 km Bücherregalen und 4000 Plätzen in den Lesesälen sorgt allein schon aufgrund seiner Größe für Aufsehen. Das Konzept vier 100 Meter hoher Türme, die wie »aufgeschlagene Bücher« rund um einen zentralen Garten angeordnet werden sollten, wurde von einer ganzen Reihe berühmter Fachleute heftig kritisiert – nicht nur wegen der offensichtlichen Nachteile bei der Lagerung von Büchern in Türmen, sondern auch aufgrund der Gefahren, denen die Bände in diesen ursprünglich sehr lichtdurchlässig konzipierten Bauten durch Licht und Wärme ausgesetzt sein würden. Daraufhin modifizierte man den Entwurf und reduzierte die Höhe der Türme, um die darin befindlichen Bücher besser zu schützen und die Größe der Magazine im Fuß des Komplexes zu steigern. Trotz eines modernen Konzepts, das zu einem Großteil der Bewunderung des Architekten für die Minimal Art und Künstler wie Carl André und Richard Serra entsprang, werden die strengen Linien der Bibliothèque durch den zentralen, versenkten Garten etwas gemildert, der vor allem von den Lesesälen aus sichtbar ist. Mit der Schaffung dieser unter Planum liegenden »grünen Borns« beabsichtigte Dominique Perrault, einen Bezug zum Garten Eden, zur Erbsünde und damit zum Usprung des Wissens herzustellen, das hier in Millionen von Büchern gelagert wird. Perrault über sein eigenes Interesse an der Kunst: »Die Architektur der Bibliothek stellt einen Versuch dar, ein Werk zu schaffen, das seiner Zeit entspricht. Die Kunstrichtungen, von denen ich mich inspirieren lasse, sind Land Art oder Minimal Art. Ich hätte dieses Gebäude gern Donald Judd gezeigt, bevor er starb. Richard Serra besuchte es, und er äußerte sich in seinen Kommentaren

le fait d'être exposés à la lumière et à la chaleur dans des bâtiments qui, au départ, devaient être presque entièrement transparents. Le projet a dû subir des modifications: la hauteur des tours a été réduite, les volumes qu'elles contiendront seront mieux protégés, et les rayons situés à la base du complexe ont été agrandis. En dépit de son concept moderniste, dû en grande partie à l'admiration que l'architecte porte à des minimalistes tels que Carl André et Richard Serra, les aspects sévères de la Bibliothèque seront quelque peu atténués par la présence du jardin central, surtout visible depuis les salles de lecture. Pour Dominique Perrault, ce nid de verdure évoque le Jardin d'Eden, le Péché originel, et, ainsi, l'origine du savoir contenu dans les millions de volumes que renferme la bibliothèque. Perrault exprime clairement son intérêt pour l'art dans ce commentaire: «L'architecture de cette bibliothèque représente une tentative de créer une œuvre appartenant à son époque. Je me suis inspiré du Land Art et du minimalisme. J'aurais aimé montrer cet édifice à Donald Judd avant sa mort. Richard Serra l'a visité, et ses commentaires ont été extrêmement positifs. A mon avis, il est grand temps que l'architecture assimile l'art de notre temps.» Interrogé sur les raisons pour lesquelles il pense que l'on devrait s'inspirer de mouvements artistiques qui ont atteint leur apogée il y a 20 ans ou plus, Dominique Perrault réplique: «20 ans, c'est justement l'intervalle de temps qui sépare l'art de l'architecture.»[11]

De nombreux critiques se sont arrêtés à la géométrie moderniste des tours, qu'ils considèrent comme dépassée en termes de réflexion architecturale. Pourtant, la personnalité imposante de la bibliothèque, particulièrement vue de l'intérieur, son gigantisme même, obligent à ne pas sous-estimer ce projet. Il ne fait aucun doute qu'une simple analyse de la géométrie de cet édifice ne suffit pas à saisir sa vraie nature. Le jardin central est un élément original, de même que l'utilisation fréquente de matériaux inhabituels tels que cette sorte de «cotte de mailles» en acier inoxydable utilisée pour les plafonds. Perrault fait lui-même remarquer que, à la différence de son jardin encastré, les édifices modernistes descendent rarement au-dessous du sol. A l'instar de la villa Savoye de Le Corbusier, ils ont plutôt tendan-

The art movements which I look to for inspiration are Land Art or Minimalism. I would like to have shown this building to Donald Judd before he died. Richard Serra did visit it, and he was extremely favorable in his comments. In my opinion, it is high time for architecture to assimilate the art of our time." When asked why he feels that art movements which reached their high point 20 years ago or more should be looked to for inspiration, Dominique Perrault responds, "Twenty years is just about the gap in time which exists between art and architecture."[11]

Many critics have retained only the Modernist geometry of the towers to criticize this project as being behind the times in terms of architectural thinking, but the strong presence of the library, especially as viewed from within, indeed its very size, make it a project to be reckoned with. There is certainly a case to be made for the fact that a simple analysis of its geometry is not sufficient to grasp the nature of this building. The central garden is an unusual aspect, as is the frequent use of materials such as a kind of "chain mail" stainless steel ceiling material within. Perrault himself points out that Modernist buildings rarely made a point of digging into the earth, as does his sunken garden. Rather, like Le Corbusier's Villa Savoye, they tended to want to rise about the ground, either on pilotis or by sitting lightly on their sites. In an almost Freudian way, Perrault claims that the Bibliothèque is far removed from the modern purist tenets, and he may be right about that. In any case, through massive intervention of the French government, a new place of intellectual gathering has been created in Paris.

Now that the library building is finished, and since François Mitterrand died in January 1996, political reasons for criticizing the Bibliothèque have ebbed, and it is being given a fair hearing, even in the foreign press. As Herbert Muschamp wrote in *The New York Times*, "I expected to hate the new Grande Bibliothèque nationale in Paris. The distant glimpses I'd had of it had already kindled my dislike. On close inspection, however, the building turns out to be both highly refined and historically aware. Dominique Perrault, the architect of this crisp and elegant composition in steel, glass and wood, has clearly taken his inspiration not

sehr zustimmend. Meiner Meinung nach wird es höchste Zeit für die Architektur, sich der Kunst unserer Zeit anzugleichen.« Auf die Frage, warum er der Meinung ist, daß man sich von Kunstrichtungen inspirieren lassen sollte, die ihren Höhepunkt bereits vor 20 Jahren erreichten, antwortet Perrault: »20 Jahre sind genau die zeitliche Kluft, die zwischen Kunst und Architektur besteht.«[11]

Viele Kritiker haben nur die modernistische Geometrie der Türme vor Augen, wenn sie dieses Projekt als nicht zeitgemäß bezeichnen, aber die starke Präsenz der Bibliothek – vor allem aus ihrem Inneren heraus betrachtet – und ihre schiere Größe machen sie zu einem Bauwerk von außergewöhnlicher Wirkung. Vieles spricht dafür, daß eine einfache Analyse der Geometrie nicht ausreicht, um die wahre Natur dieses Gebäudes zu erfassen. Der zentrale Garten ist ein ebenso ungewöhnlicher Aspekt wie die häufige Verwendung unüblicher Materialien wie etwa einer Art »Kettenpanzer« aus Edelstahl als Deckenverkleidung im Gebäudeinneren. Perrault selbst weist darauf hin, daß es kein Kennzeichen der Moderne war, so tief in die Erde zu bauen wie im Falle seines Gartens. Statt dessen – wie etwa bei Le Corbusiers Villa Savoye – neigte man dazu, sich über den Erdboden zu erheben, entweder auf Pfeilern oder mit möglichst geringem Bodenkontakt. Auf eine nahezu Freudsche Weise behauptet Perrault, die Bibliothèque sei weit von modernen, puristischen Grundsätzen entfernt – und er könnte damit Recht haben. Auf jeden Fall ist mit Hilfe massiver Intervention der französischen Regierung mitten in Paris ein neuer Ort intellektueller Sammlung entstanden.

Nach der Fertigstellung der Bibliothèque und seit François Mitterrands Tod im Januar 1996 ist die politisch motivierte Kritik abgeebbt, und Perraults Bauwerk erhält jetzt endlich eine faire Berichterstattung – sogar in der Auslandspresse. Herbert Muschamp schrieb in der »New York Times«: »Ich ging davon aus, daß ich die neue Bibliothèque nationale in Paris hassen würde. Die flüchtigen Blicke, die ich darauf geworfen hatte, entfachten meine Abneigung. Bei näherer Betrachtung erwies sich das Bauwerk jedoch als ebenso kultiviert wie historisch bewußt.

ce à s'élever au-dessus du sol, soit sur des pilotis, soit sur une
assise légère. D'une manière presque freudienne, Perrault soutient que la Bibliothèque est très éloignée des principes des
puristes modernes, et il a peut-être raison. Dans tous les cas,
grâce à l'intervention appuyée du gouvernement français, Paris
s'enrichit d'un nouveau lieu de culture.

La Bibliothèque est aujourd'hui achevée, et, depuis la dispari-
tion de François Mitterrand en janvier 1996, il existe moins de
raisons politiques de critiquer cet ouvrage. Aujourd'hui, il reçoit
un accueil plus impartial, même dans la presse étrangère.
Ainsi, Herbert Muschamp écrit dans «The New York Times»:
«Je m'attendais à détester la Grande Bibliothèque nationale.
Les visions fugitives et lointaines que j'en avais eu m'avaient
d'abord déplu. Toutefois, après un examen minutieux, cet édifice
s'avère très raffiné et riche d'une épaisseur historique. Il est clair
que Dominique Perrault, l'auteur de cette élégante composition
d'acier, de verre et de bois, s'est inspiré du style international et
de l'art minimal des années 1960 et 1970. La disposition symétrique des quatre tours rappelle le classicisme radical qui a pré-
cédé la chute de l'Ancien Régime.»[12]

Nous terminerons cette revue des bâtiments institutionnels
récemment construits en France par la Cour européenne des
droits de l'homme à Strasbourg. Ce bâtiment a été conçu par
Richard Rogers avec l'aide de Renzo Piano, architecte du Centre
Georges Pompidou à Paris (1977). Inaugurée officiellement le
29 juin 1995, la Cour est une émanation de la Convention européenne de sauvegarde des droits de l'homme et des libertés
fondamentales (Rome, 4 nov. 1950), appliquée depuis 1953. En
principe, les deux divisions de cette organisation (la Commission et la Cour des droits de l'homme) sont à la disposition des
personnes qui pensent que leurs droits fondamentaux ont été
violés. Etablie à Strasbourg depuis 1962, dans un bâtiment de
3800 m², la Cour s'est vu concéder par la ville un terrain de deux
hectares, et une résolution du Conseil des ministres européens
(26 avril 1986) l'a chargée d'y faire construire un nouvel édifice
de 20 000 m². L'inauguration officielle était prévue le 5 mai 1989,
mais elle a dû être reportée, en partie parce que les plans propo-

Richard Rogers, European Court of Human Rights, Strasbourg, France, 1989–95, view on the Ill River.

Richard Rogers, Europäischer Gerichtshof für Menschenrechte, Straßburg, Frankreich, 1989–95. Blick auf den Fluß Ill.

Richard Rogers, Cour européenne des droits de l'homme, Strasbourg, France, 1989–95. Vue sur la rivière Ill.

only from the International Style, but also from minimal art of the 1960s and 70s. In their symmetry, the library's four towers recall the radical classicism that preceded the downfall of the ancien régime."[12]

A final institutional structure built recently in France is the European Court of Human Rights in Strasbourg, designed by Richard Rogers, well known in the country for his design, with Renzo Piano, of the Centre Georges Pompidou in Paris (1977). Officially inaugurated on June 29, 1995, the European Court is an outgrowth of the European Convention on Human Rights, signed in Rome on November 4, 1950, and applied since 1953. Through two branches, the Commission and the Court of Human Rights, this organization is in principle at the disposition of those persons who feel that their guaranteed human rights have been violated. Based in a 3,800 m² building in Strasbourg since 1962, the

Dominique Perrault, der Architekt dieser klaren und eleganten Komposition in Stahl, Glas und Holz, hat sich bei seinem Entwurf deutlich nicht nur vom International Style, sondern auch von der Minimal Art der 60er und 70er Jahre inspirieren lassen. In ihrer Symmetrie lassen die vier Türme der Bibliothek den radikalen Klassizismus wiederauferstehen, der den Niedergang des ancien régime ankündigte.«[12]

Das letzte der kürzlich in Frankreich entstandenen institutionellen Bauwerke ist der Europäische Gerichtshof für Menschenrechte in Straßburg. Verantwortlicher Architekt ist Richard Rogers, der in Frankreich für seinen – zusammen mit Renzo Piano erstellten – Entwurf des Centre Georges Pompidou in Paris (1977) berühmt wurde. Der offiziell am 29. Juni 1995 eingeweihte Europäische Gerichtshof ging aus dem Europäischen Abkommen über die Menschenrechte hervor, das am 4. November 1950 in Rom unterzeichnet wurde und seit 1953 in Kraft ist. Mit seinen beiden Abteilungen, der Kommission und dem Gerichtshof für Menschenrechte, steht diese Organisation all denen zur Verfügung, die der Meinung sind, daß ihre garantierten Menschenrechte verletzt wurden. Nach einem Beschluß des Europäischen Ministerrats vom 26. April 1986 wurde dem seit 1962 in einem 3800 m² großen Gebäude in Straßburg angesiedelten Gerichtshof ein 2 Hektar großes Grundstück bewilligt, auf dem ein neuer, 20 000 m² großer Komplex entstehen sollte. Das ursprünglich geplante Einweihungsdatum, der 5. Mai 1989, konnte nicht aufrechterhalten werden – nicht zuletzt deshalb, weil sich die vorliegenden Entwürfe der Architekten als ungenügend herausgestellt hatten. Die Stadt Straßburg, die das Baugelände zur Verfügung stellte, schrieb einen Wettbewerb aus, und am 19. September 1989 wurde Richard Rogers ausgewählt. Rogers hatte einen geschwungenen, zweiteiligen Entwurf eingereicht, der der zweigliedrigen Funktionsweise der Organisation entsprach. Als man sich für Rogers entschied, sollte das auf 240 Millionen Francs veranschlagte Vorhaben Raum für 25 Mitgliedstaaten bieten. Mit dem Fall der Berliner Mauer erhöhte sich deren Zahl jedoch auf 34, so daß das Projekt im Frühjahr 1992 um 3000 m² neue Büroflächen erweitert wurde. So wuchsen die

sés manquaient d'inspiration. La municipalité de Strasbourg a organisé un concours, et Richard Rogers a été choisi le 19 septembre 1989. Il proposait un bâtiment arrondi et bicéphale reflétant la nature bipartite de l'organisation. A l'époque, le coût de construction estimé à 240 millions de francs correspondait à une installation conçue pour 25 pays membres. Mais, avec la chute du mur de Berlin, ce nombre est passé à 34, et, au cours du printemps 1992, 3000 m² de bureaux supplémentaires ont dû être ajoutés au projet. En décembre 1994, le coût total s'élevait à 455 millions de francs. Le projet final prévoyait un édifice de 28 000 m², dont 860 m² consacrés à la salle d'audience, 520 m² à la salle de réunion de la Commission, 4500 m² aux différentes salles de réunion, et 16 500 m² aux bureaux.

Il faut noter que le «Protocole 11», signé par tous les Etats membres depuis le 11 mai 1994 et déjà ratifié par neuf d'entre eux, précise que l'organisation aujourd'hui bipartite sera dissoute au profit d'une structure comportant une seule cour. Ainsi, sans que Richard Rogers puisse être tenu pour responsable, le symbolisme de son projet ne correspond plus au fonctionnement réel de la Cour européenne des droits de l'homme.

Des formes d'art

Même si quelques architectes comme Ben van Berkel semblent rejeter l'assimilation artistes/architectes – tendance qui semble s'affirmer –, d'autres l'adoptent volontiers. De fait, la liberté avec laquelle l'architecture a pu tirer son inspiration de l'art est un des événements les plus importants de ces dernières années. Des architectes non-européens tels que le Californien Frank O. Gehry ont peut-être joué un rôle essentiel dans cette transition mais, en Europe, cette tendance s'est imposée comme un phénomène indépendant. L'Italien Massimiliano Fuksas compte parmi les exégètes les plus convaincants des liens entre l'art et l'architecture dans le but d'enrichir la création. Les résultats de ses recherches sont visibles à l'entrée de la grotte de Niaux et à l'école des beaux-arts de Bordeaux. «Je crois que plus l'architecture contemporaine avance, plus elle ressemble à la sculpture, affirme-t-il. L'influence de l'art sur l'architecture est bien plus

Court was granted a 2 hectare plot of land, and asked to build a new 20,000 m² building by a resolution of the European Council of Ministers on April 26, 1986. The initially planned date for the inauguration, May 5, 1989 was not maintained, partially because the proposed architectural plans were found lacking. The city of Strasbourg, which granted the land, then organized a competition, and Richard Rogers was chosen on September 19, 1989. Rogers proposed a curved, double-headed building, corresponding to the bi-partite function of the organization. When Rogers was chosen, the 240 million French franc construction cost corresponded to facilities for 25 member states, but with the fall of the Berlin Wall, that number increased to 34, and 3,000 m² of new office space were added to the project in the spring of 1992. The final cost increased to 455 million French francs by December 1994. The final project, a 28,000 m² structure, includes 860 m² for the main court room, 520 m² for the meeting room of the Commission, 4,500 m² of meeting rooms, and 16,500 m² for the offices.

It should be noted that the so-called "Protocol 11" signed by all of the member states since May 11, 1994 and already ratified by nine of them, provides that the current bi-partite organization will be dissolved in favor of a unique court structure. Through no fault of his own, the very symbolism of Richard Rogers's building thus no longer corresponds to the actual functioning of the European Court of Human Rights.

Forms of Art

Although some architects like Ben van Berkel seem to reject the assimilation of artists and architects which seems to be a strong trend, others happily embrace it. The freedom enjoyed by architecture to draw on art as a source is indeed one of the important events which have occurred in recent years. Non-Europeans like the California architect Frank O. Gehry may have played a leading role in permitting this transition, but within Europe, this has now become a strong, independent trend. One of the more articulate proponents of links between art and architecture as a way of enriching design is the Italian Massimiliano Fuksas. The results of his investigation can be seen in the recent Niaux

Gesamtkosten bis zum Dezember 1994 auf 455 Millionen Francs an. Das Projekt umfaßt in seiner endgültigen Form 28 000 m², davon 860 m² für den großen Gerichtssaal, 520 m² für den Sitzungssaal der Kommission, 4 500 m² für die übrigen Konferenzräume und 16 500 m² für die Büros. Ironischerweise sieht das seit dem 11. Mai 1994 von allen Mitgliedstaaten unterzeichnete 11. Zusatzprotokoll vor, daß die zweigliedrige Organisation des Gerichts durch eine einheitliche Gerichtsorganisation abgelöst werden soll. Die von Rogers eigens für dieses Bauwerk entwickelte Symbolik entspricht somit nicht mehr der gegenwärtigen Organisationsform des Europäischen Gerichtshofs für Menschenrechte, wenngleich der Architekt hierfür nicht verantwortlich zu machen ist.

Formen der Kunst

Obwohl einige Architekten, wie etwa Ben van Berkel, eine Angleichung von Künstlern und Architekten ablehnen, nehmen andere diesen zur Zeit starken Trend mit offenen Armen auf. Eines der wichtigsten Merkmale der vergangenen Jahre ist in der Tat die neugewonnene Freiheit der Architektur, auch künstlerische Tendenzen als Inspirationsquelle heranzuziehen. Während Nicht-Europäer wie Frank O. Gehry in diesem Übergangsstadium eine führende Rolle gespielt haben mögen, bildet sich innerhalb Europas erst jetzt ein starker, unabhängiger Trend heraus. Einer der erklärten Verfechter der Verbindung von Kunst und Architektur als Mittel zur Bereicherung der Entwurfsmöglichkeiten ist der italienische Architekt Massimiliano Fuksas. Die Ergebnisse seiner Studien lassen sich an dem vor kurzem fertiggestellten Eingang zur Niaux-Grotte und der Kunstschule der Université Michel de Montaigne in Bordeaux ablesen. Fuksas vertritt die Ansicht, daß »die Architektur, je weiter sie sich entwickelt, immer mehr der Bildhauerei ähnelt. [...] Auf jeden Fall ist der Einfluß der Kunst auf die Architektur heute erheblich größer als etwa in den 70er Jahren.« An welcher Kunstdisziplin orientiert sich ein Architekt wie Massimiliano Fuksas? »Ich persönlich interessiere mich für Joseph Beuys aufgrund seines sehr ausgeprägten moralischen Empfindens für den sozialen Nutzen der

Richard Rogers, European Court of Human Rights, Strasbourg, France, 1989–95. View looking from one of the office wings toward the entrance.

Richard Rogers, Europäischer Gerichtshof für Menschenrechte, Straßburg, Frankreich, 1989–95. Blick aus einem der Büroflügel auf den Eingangsbereich.

Richard Rogers, Cour européenne des droits de l'homme, Strasbourg, France, 1989–95. Vue depuis l'une des ailes de bureaux, vers l'entrée.

importante aujourd'hui que dans les années 1970 par exemple.» Vers quelle sorte d'art un architecte comme Massimiliano Fuksas se tourne-t-il? «Personnellement, répond-il, je m'intéresse à Joseph Beuys parce que je vois derrière l'utilité sociale de l'art qu'il défendait un formidable sens moral.» L'exemple de Beuys, dont l'influence s'est surtout fait sentir il y a plus de 20 ans, semble indiquer qu'un certain laps de temps sépare l'art et l'architecture. «Les architectes sont vraiment en retard, dit Fuksas. Dans les années 1940 et 1950, quand le style international se vidait de sa substance, nous avons perdu beaucoup de temps. Ce n'est qu'à la fin des années 1970 que l'on a commencé à s'efforcer de recréer des liens entre les différents types d'expression artistique, y compris l'architecture.» Interrogé sur la façon dont architectes et artistes se sont rapprochés ces dernières années, Fuksas répond: «Auparavant, les architectes considéraient que la vie quotidienne les concernait peu. Leur rôle consistait à donner leur avis, à dire aux autres comment ils devaient vivre. Aujourd'hui, il faudrait être stupide pour voir les choses ainsi. Cette prise de conscience signifie que artistes et architectes jouent un rôle beaucoup plus important parce qu'ils sont de nouveau en contact direct avec la façon de vivre des gens.»[13]

Dernièrement, Zaha Hadid et Enric Miralles, deux personnalités de notoriété internationale qui ont été en contact avec l'Architectural Association à Londres, ont prouvé qu'il existe une nouvelle approche de l'architecture, où le créateur est libre de s'aventurer davantage vers un mode sculptural. La caserne de pompiers Vitra (1988–93), située à Weil am Rhein (Allemagne) est l'une des premières œuvres de Zaha Hadid. Elle montre bien que les dessins spectaculaires de cette architecte peuvent devenir des bâtiments réalisables. Bien qu'elle ait été étiquetée comme «déconstructiviste», Hadid imprime à ses formes fragmentées un dynamisme très personnel.

Installé à Barcelone, Enric Miralles est allé encore plus loin que Hadid dans la conception de son sculptural Centre de méditation Unazuki (1991–93), à Toyama (Japon). Il le décrit ainsi: «Un pont, un petit parc et un sentier de vieux pèlerin fusionnent

Massimiliano Fuksas, Cave Entrance, Niaux, France, 1988–93. Sculptural wings in Corten steel.

Massimiliano Fuksas, Höhleneingang zur Niaux-Grotte, Frankreich, 1988–93. Skulpturale Flügel aus Corten-Stahl.

Massimiliano Fuksas, Entrée de la grotte de Niaux, France, 1988–93. Ailes sculpturales en acier corten.

Cave Entrance, and Bordeaux Art School. "I believe that the more contemporary architecture goes forward, the more it resembles sculpture", says Fuksas. "In any case," he continues, "the influence of art on architecture is much greater today than it was in the 1970s for example." What sort of art does an architect like Massimiliano Fuksas look toward? "Personally" he answers, "I am interested in Joseph Beuys because of the very strong moral sense of the social usefulness of art which he defended." The example of Beuys, whose influence was felt most over 20 years ago, again seems to indicate a time gap between art and architecture. "Architects are definitely behind the times," says Fuksas. "As the International Style was emptied of its substance in the 1940s and 1950s, we lost a lot of time," he continues. "It was only in the late 1970s that the first efforts were made to recreate new links between the different types of artistic expression including architecture." When asked how architects and artists have been brought closer together in recent years,

Kunst, als dessen Verteidiger er auftrat.« Die Tatsache, daß Fuksas Beuys erwähnt, dessen Einfluß vor etwa zwanzig Jahren am deutlichsten zu spüren war, deutet erneut auf eine zeitliche Kluft zwischen Kunst und Architektur hin. »Die Architektur hinkt definitiv der Zeit hinterher«, erklärt Fuksas. »Als der International Style in den 40er und 50er Jahren seiner Substanz beraubt wurde, haben wir viel Zeit verloren. Erst gegen Ende der 70er Jahre unternahm man die ersten Versuche, wieder neue Verbindungen zwischen verschiedenen Formen künstlerischen Ausdrucks – einschließlich der Architektur – zu schaffen.« Auf die Frage, auf welchem Wege Künstler und Architekten in den vergangenen Jahren einander nähergebracht wurden, antwortet Fuksas: »Früher vertraten die Architekten die Ansicht, daß sie sehr wenig mit dem alltäglichen Leben zu tun haben sollten. Ihre Aufgabe war es, Urteile abzugeben und anderen zu sagen, wie sie zu leben hatten. Heutzutage erwägen nur Narren eine solche Haltung. Aber diese Feststellung an sich bedeutet, daß Künstler und Architekten sehr viel wichtiger geworden sind, da sie erneut in direktem Kontakt zur Lebensweise der meisten Menschen stehen.«[13]

Zwei internationale Persönlichkeiten der Architekturwelt, Zaha Hadid und Enric Miralles, haben vor kurzem bewiesen, daß ein neuer Architekturansatz existiert, der es dem Künstler gestattet, sich intensiver mit einer skulpturalen Formensprache zu beschäftigen. Zaha Hadids Feuerwehrhaus der Firma Vitra in Weil am Rhein (1988–93) ist eines der ersten von ihr fertiggestellten Bauwerke und beweist, daß ihre aufsehenerregenden Zeichnungen tatsächlich in funktionsfähige Gebäude umgesetzt werden können. Obwohl man sie den »Dekonstruktivisten« zuordnete, besitzen Hadids fragmentarische Formen eine sehr persönliche Dynamik. Der in Barcelona tätige Enric Miralles ging mit dem skulpturalen Entwurf seines Unazuki-Meditationszentrums in Toyama (1991–93) sogar noch einen Schritt weiter. Miralles erklärt: »Eine Brücke, ein kleiner Park und ein alter Pilgerpfad wurden vereinigt und aufeinander abgestimmt, um dieses Ensemble zu bilden, das als eine Einheit mit der rauhen Schönheit der Natur erfahren wird.«[14] Eine verblüffende

et s'adaptent les uns aux autres pour former cet ensemble ressenti comme une union avec la beauté sauvage de la nature.»[14] Une surprenante arabesque de tubes d'acier encercle une plate-forme, combinant architecture et art *in situ* pour créer un ensemble convaincant.

Ces références à l'architecture en tant qu'art sont symptomatiques du dynamisme qui anime les créations européennes récentes. Dominique Perrault a peut-être raison en affirmant que l'architecture a pris un peu de retard par rapport à la liberté créatrice de l'art. En essayant de créer une rupture avec le poids de la tradition, les Européens, au début du XXe siècle, ont été les précurseurs du style international qui devait dominer l'architecture pendant une bonne partie du siècle. Pourtant, c'est aux Etats-Unis que cette forme de modernisme a acquis son nom et son vocabulaire formaliste. Pendant la reconstruction de l'Europe dévastée par la guerre, le modernisme était opportun. Ses lignes géométriques et les matériaux modernes utilisés permettaient de construire rapidement et à peu de frais. Toutefois, en passant par l'Amérique, le mouvement moderne a perdu son caractère radical. Le style international n'était plus qu'une coquille vide lorsque, dans les années 1970, les Américains ont lancé la mode postmoderne, qui ne fut rien de plus qu'une impulsion décorative. Les ouvrages présentés dans ce volume montrent bien que les architectes européens ont intégré non seulement leur passé lointain, mais aussi les conquêtes intellectuelles et techniques de la période moderne. Le sens des responsabilités et la fièvre inventive exprimés par Ben van Berkel indiquent bien la présence d'une nouvelle vague européenne qui permet une fois de plus au moderne de s'affirmer comme nouveau.

Massimiliano Fuksas, Bordeaux Art School, Bordeaux, France, 1993–94. With cladding in oxidized copper.

Massimiliano Fuksas, Kunstschule der Université Michel de Montaigne in Bordeaux, Frankreich, 1993–94. Verkleidung aus oxidiertem Kupfer.

Massimiliano Fuksas, Ecole des beaux-arts de Bordeaux, France, 1993–94. Revêtement en cuivre oxydé vert clair.

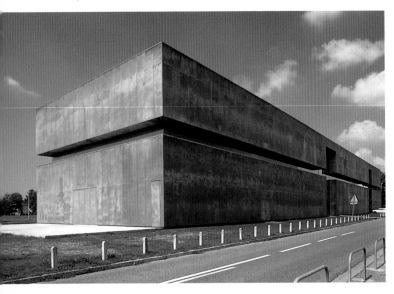

Fuksas replies, "Before, architects considered that they should have very little to do with day to day life. They were there to give their judgments, to tell others how to live. Today, you would have to be a fool to have such an attitude. But that discovery in itself means that artists and architects have become much more important because they are once again in direct contact with the way people live."[13]

Two international figures who have had contact with the Architectural Association in London, Zaha Hadid and Enric Miralles, have recently given proof that a new approach to architecture exists, which frees the designer to delve much more into a sculptural mode. Zaha Hadid's Vitra fire Station, located in Weil am Rhein, Germany (1988–93) is one of her first built works, and proof that her spectacular drawings can indeed be translated into workable buildings. Although she has been labeled a "deconstructivist" architect, Hadid's own fragmented forms have a very personal dynamism. Enric Miralles, who is based in Barcelona has gone even further than Hadid in designing his sculptural Unazuki Meditation Center in Toyama, Japan (1991–93). According to the architect, "A bridge, a small park and an old pilgrim's path are unified and attuned to each other to form this ensemble, experienced as a union with the rugged

Arabeske aus Stahlröhren umschließt eine Aussichtsplattform und vereint Architektur und geländespezifische Kunst zu einem überzeugenden Ganzen.

Diese Verweise auf die Architektur als Kunstform sind symptomatisch für die Dynamik der jüngsten europäischen Entwürfe. Architekten wie Perrault und Fuksas mögen Recht haben mit ihrer These, die Architektur hinke, im Vergleich zur kreativen Freiheit der Kunst, ihrer Zeit hinterher. In dem Bemühen, zu Beginn des Jahrhunderts einen völligen Bruch mit der schweren Last der Tradition zu bewirken, legten die europäischen Architekten das Fundament für den International Style, der die Architektur während eines Großteils des 20. Jahrhunderts beherrschen sollte. Dennoch erhielt diese Form der Moderne ihren Namen und ihre architektonische Formensprache in den Vereinigten Staaten. Während des Wiederaufbaus im vom Krieg zerstörten Europa stellte die Moderne ein Mittel zum Zweck dar: ihre geometrischen Linien und modernen Materialien gestatteten eine preiswerte und zügige Bauweise. Dennoch hatte der Weg durch Amerika die Moderne ihrer radikalen Botschaft beraubt. In den 70er Jahren war der International Style nichts weiter als eine leere Hülle, als die Amerikaner die Postmoderne lancierten, die kaum mehr als einen dekorativen Impuls darstellte. Die in diesem Buch vorgestellten Projekte künden von einer Assimilation europäischer Architekten – nicht nur ihrer weit zurückliegenden Vergangenheit, sondern auch der intellektuellen und technischen Errungenschaften der Moderne. Das von Ben van Berkel zum Ausdruck gebrachte Verantwortungsgefühl und die Freude an der Innovation sind Anzeichen einer Bewegung innerhalb der europäischen Architektur, die es der Moderne erlaubt, sich wieder zu erneuern.

Massimiliano Fuksas, Bordeaux Art School, Bordeaux,
France, 1993–94. Painting by the architect.

Massimiliano Fuksas, Kunstschule der Université
Michel de Montaigne in Bordeaux, Frankreich,
1993–94. Gemälde des Architekten.

Massimiliano Fuksas, Ecole des beaux-arts de
Bordeaux, France, 1993–94. Peinture de l'architecte.

beauty of nature."[14] A surprising arabesque of steel tubes
encircles a viewing platform, integrating architecture and
site-specific art into a convincing whole.

These references to architecture as art are symptomatic of the
dynamism encountered in recent European designs. Architects
like Perrault and Fuksas may be right in saying that architecture
is somewhat behind the times as compared to the creative
liberty of art. Having sought to create a complete break with
the weight of tradition early in the century, the Europeans laid
the groundwork for the International Style which was to domi-
nate architecture for a good part of the 20th century. And yet,
it was in the United States that this form of Modernism was
given its name and assumed its formalist vocabulary. During
the reconstruction of war-torn Europe, Modernism was a means
to an end. Its geometric lines and modern materials permitted
inexpensive rapid construction. Yet its passage through America
had somehow emptied the modern of its radical message.
The International Style was no more than an empty shell in the
1970s when the Americans launched the Post-Modern fashion,
itself little more than a decorative impulse. The projects present-
ed in this volume signify an assimilation by European architects
not only of their more distant past, but also of the intellectual
and technical conquests of the modern period.

The sense of responsibility and the excitement of invention
expressed by Ben van Berkel are signs of a wave in European
architecture which permits the modern to once again be new.

Notes / Anmerkungen

1 "Centre galicien d'art contemporain," interview of Alvaro Siza, *L'Architecture
d'aujourd'hui*, 1994.

2 Millot, Lorraine, "Berlin-chantier désespère de devenir une capitale,"
Libération, October 22, 1995.

3 *Der Spiegel*, 51/1993, page 51.

4 *Arch+*, 121, March 1994.

5 Curtis, William, "Juha Leiviskä," *L'Architecture d'aujourd'hui*, October 1995.

6 Interview of Ben van Berkel, van berkel & bos, Amsterdam, October 1995.

7 Ibid.

8 Ibid.

9 Dietsch, Deborah, "Preservation Needs Better Architecture," Editorial,
Architecture, November 1995.

10 Pisani, Mario, "Architecture Studio, Rites de Passage," Wordsearch
Publishing, Carte Segrete, Rome, 1995.

11 Perrault, Dominique, interview, February 3, 1995.

12 Muschamp, Herbert, "Challenging the All-Too Rational,"
The New York Times, December 31, 1995.

13 Fuksas, Massimiliano, interview, Paris, October 12, 1995.

14 Miralles, Enric, in: *El Croquis*, 72 (II), Madrid, 1995.

Bibliography | Bibliographie

Adjmi, Morris (ed.): *Aldo Rossi, The Complete Buildings and Projects, 1981–1991*. Thames & Hudson. London, 1992

Art and Power, Europe under the dictators, 1930–45. Exhibition catalogue compiled and selected by Dawn Ades, Tim Benton, David Elliot, Jan Boyd Whyte. Hayward Gallery, 1995

Augé, Marc: *L'usine L'Oréal, Denis Valode, Jean Pistre.* Collection Un Lieu/Un Architecte. Les Editions du Demi-Cercle. Paris, 1995

Balfour, Alan (ed.): *World Cities. Berlin.* Academy Editions. London, 1995

Ben van Berkel: in *El Croquis*, 72 (I). Madrid, 1995

Bibliothèque Nationale de France 1989–1995. Birkhäuser. Basel, 1995

Cohn, David: *Pilgrimage to Santiago, Galician Center of Contemporary Art.* in: *Architectural Record.* October 1994

Deutsches Architekturmuseum (ed.): *Architektur Jahrbuch 1992, 1993, 1994.* Prestel. Munich

Dos Santos, José Paulo (ed.): *Alvaro Siza, Works and Projects, 1954–1992.* Gustavo Gili, Barcelona, 1993

Edelmann, Frédéric: *Berlin veut s'imposer comme «le plus grand chantier du monde».* In: *Le Monde.* July 7, 1995

Emanuel, Muriel (ed.): *Contemporary Architects.* St. James Press. 3rd edition. New York, 1994

Embassy of Finland, Washington, D.C. in: *Architecture and Urbanism A+U.* A+U Publishing. Tokyo, July 1995

Feireiss, Kristin (ed.): *Ben van Berkel, Mobile Forces.* Ernst & Sohn. Berlin, 1994

Feldmeyer, Gerhard: *The New German Architecture.* Rizzoli. New York, 1993

Massimiliano Fuksas. Artemis. Zurich, 1994

Zaha Hadid. in: *El Croquis*, 73 (I). Madrid, 1995

Juha Leiviskä. in: *Architecture and Urbanism A+U.* A+U Publishing. Tokyo, April 1995

Llano, Pedro de and **Castanheira,** Carlos (ed.): *Alvaro Siza, Works and Projects.* Electa Espana. Centro Galego de Arte Contemporanea, Santiago de Compostela, 1995

Millot, Lorraine: *Berlin – chantier désespère de devenir une capitale.* in: *Libération,* October 22, 1995

Enric Miralles. in: *El Croquis*, 72 (II). Madrid, 1995

Enric Miralles. in: *Architectural Monograph No 10.* Academy Editions. London, 1995

Peter Blum Edition (ed.): *Architectures of Herzog & de Meuron.* New York, 1994

Dominique Perrault. Artemis. Zurich, 1994

Petit, Jean: *Botta, traces d'architecture.* Fidia Edizioni d'Arte. Lugano, 1994

Pisani, Mario: *Architecture Studio, rites de passage.* Wordsearch Publishing, Carte Segrete. Rom, 1995

Powell, Kenneth: *Richard Rogers.* Artemis. London, 1994

Quantrill, Malcolm: *Finnish Architecture and the Modernist Tradition.* Chapman & Hall. London, 1995

Richard Rogers. Tensile Structures. in: *AD Architectural Design.* London, 1995

Schweger + Partner: *Kunstmuseum Wolfsburg.* Aedes, Galerie und Architekturforum. Berlin, 1993

Scully, Vincent and **Moneo,** Rafael (essays): *Aldo Rossi.* Rizzoli. New York, 1985

Sudjic, Deyan: *The Architecture of Richard Rogers.* Wordsearch. London, 1994

Trigueiros, Luiz (ed.): *Alvaro Siza.* Editorial Blau. Lisbon, 1995

Tzonis, Alexander and **Lefaivre,** Liane: *Architecture in Europe since 1968.* Thames and Hudson. London, 1992

Tzonis, Alexander and **Lefaivre,** Liane: *Movement, Structure and the Work of Santiago Calatrava.* Birkhäuser. Basle, 1995

Venturi, Robert: *Complexity and Contradiction in Architecture.* The Museum of Modern Art. New York, 1966

Page 59: Enric Miralles, Unazuki Meditation Center, Toyama, Japan, 1991–93, an architecture which verges on sculpture. Pages 60/61: Zaha Hadid, Vitra Fire Station, Weil am Rhein, Germany, 1988–93. One of the few built works by this important architect.

Seite 59: Enric Miralles, Unazuki-Meditationszentrum, Toyama, Japan, 1991–93. Eine Architektur an der Grenze zur Skulptur. Seite 60/61: Zaha Hadid, Feuerwehrhaus der Firma Vitra, Weil am Rhein, Deutschland, 1988–93. Eines der wenigen realisierten Bauwerke dieser bedeutenden Architektin.

Page 59: Enric Miralles, Centre de méditation Unazuki, Toyama, Japon, 1991–93. Une architecture confinant à la sculpture. Pages 60/61: Zaha Hadid, Caserne de pompiers de Vitra, Weil am Rhein, Allemagne, 1988–93. L'une des rares œuvres de ce grand architecte.

Architecture Studio

In the description of their firm, the partners of Architecture Studio, Rodo Tisnado, Martin Robain, Alain Bretagnolle, René-Henri Arnaud, Jean-François Bonne and Laurent-Marc Fischer, use the words "up-to-date, extreme and avant-garde." They also insist on the rigorous approach of this unusual partnership which eschews the personalized "star system" now prevalent in contemporary architecture. Especially in the early phases of their work, they may have suffered from this self-imposed group image. Although they played a part in the design of the Institut du Monde Arabe (1981–87) in Paris, for example, it was Jean Nouvel who garnered most of the credit. Often futuristic in form, their work embodies an optimism or a confidence in new shapes which runs against a good part of the current architectural scene, yet they have succeeded in obtaining major commissions such as the new 180,000 m² European Parliament building in Strasbourg (1994–97).

Bei der Beschreibung ihrer Firma bedienen sich die Partner des Architecture Studio – Rodo Tisnado, Martin Robain, Alain Bretagnolle, René-Henri Arnaud, Jean François Bonne und Laurent-Marc Fischer – der Begriffe »modern, extremistisch und avantgardistisch«. Darüber hinaus beharrt diese ungewöhnliche Partnerschaft auf ihrer rigorosen Einstellung, das personalisierte »Star-System« der heutigen Architekturszene bewußt vermeiden zu wollen – wobei es denkbar ist, daß ihnen dieses selbstgewählte Image, vor allem in den Anfangsjahren, eher geschadet hat. Denn obwohl Architecture Studio am Entwurf des Institut du Monde Arabe (1981–87) in Paris beteiligt war, strich Jean Nouvel den Großteil der Anerkennung ein. Häufig futuristisch in der Form, verkörpern die Bauten des Architecture Studio einen Optimismus und ein Vertrauen in neue Formen, das die Mehrheit der heutigen Architekturszene nicht teilen kann. Dennoch ist es der Gruppe gelungen, den Zuschlag für Großaufträge wie das neue, 180 000 m² große Gebäude des Europäischen Parlaments in Straßburg (1994–97) zu erhalten.

Les associés d'Architecture Studio – Rodo Tisnado, Martin Robain, Alain Bretagnolle, René-Henri Arnaud, Jean-François Bonne et Laurent-Marc Fischer – présentent leur agence comme «moderne», «extrémiste» et «avant-gardiste». L'approche rigoureuse de cette association peu commune leur permet d'éviter de tomber dans le «star system» qui prévaut aujourd'hui dans l'architecture contemporaine. A leurs débuts surtout, ils ont peut-être souffert de l'image de groupe qu'ils se sont donnée. Ainsi, bien qu'ils aient pris part à la conception de l'Institut du monde arabe à Paris (1981–87), c'est surtout Jean Nouvel qui en a récolté le mérite. Par leurs lignes souvent futuristes, leurs ouvrages incarnent un optimisme et une confiance dans les nouvelles formes qui va à l'encontre de ce que l'on voit présenté aujourd'hui sur la scène de l'architecture. Toutefois, ils ont obtenu des commandes de première importance, parmi lesquelles le nouveau bâtiment du Parlement européen de Strasbourg (1994–97; 180000 m²). ·

Lycée Jules Verne, Cergy-Le-Haut, France, 1991–93.

Lycée Jules Verne, Cergy-Le-Haut, Frankreich, 1991–93.

Lycée Jules Verne, Cergy-le-Haut, France, 1991–93.

Lycée Jules Verne

Cergy-le-Haut, France, 1991–1993

This is a 16,600 m² facility for 1,350 pupils built with a budget of 108 million French francs. Architecture Studio was chosen in a 1991 competition organized by the Ile de France Regional Council. At that time they had already proven their capacity to build a futuristic school, with their 1987 Lycée du Futur in the Futuroscope park near Poitiers. The Lycée Jules Verne, near the Mirapolis amusement park, is set on a restrictive triangular site. The cylindrical building in the main body of the triangle houses staff facilities, and a series of bridges join the different volumes together. Parking spaces for 78 vehicles are included in the structure. Aerodynamic in both plan and section, the Lycée Jules Verne demonstrates a faith in modern forms which architects in some other countries seem to have abandoned. Despite the science-fiction aspects of this design, well-attuned to the name which it carries, the architects cite the French high-speed train, the TGV, as being a design influence.

Bei dem 16600 m² großen Komplex handelt es sich um ein für 1350 Schüler entworfenes Gebäude, das mit einem Budget von 108 Millionen Francs realisiert wurde. Aus einem vom Conseil Régional Ile de France 1991 ausgeschriebenen Wettbewerb ging das Büro Architecture Studio als Sieger hervor, das 1987 mit seinem Lycée du Futur im Futuroscope-Freizeitpark in der Nähe von Poitiers bereits seine Fähigkeiten im Entwurf futuristischer Schulgebäude unter Beweis gestellt hatte. Das Lycée Jules Verne liegt in der Nähe des Mirapolis-Freizeitparks auf einem relativ beengten, dreieckigen Grundstück. In dem zylindrischen Baukörper im Hauptteil des Dreiecks befinden sich die Räume für Lehrkörper und Personal; die einzelnen Baukörper sind durch Brücken untereinander verbunden. Darüber hinaus bietet der Komplex Parkmöglichkeiten für 78 Fahrzeuge. Das in Profil und Grundriß aerodynamische Lycée Jules Verne offenbart ein Vertrauen in moderne Formen, das bei Architekten anderer Länder scheinbar nicht mehr existiert. Trotz der Science-Fiction-Reminiszenzen des Entwurfs, die gut zum Namen des Gebäudes passen, geben die Architekten an, sie seien bei der Formgebung durch den französischen Hochgeschwindigkeitszug TGV beeinflußt worden.

Ce complexe de 16600 m² destiné à accueillir 1350 élèves a coûté 108 millions de francs. Architecture Studio a remporté le concours organisé en 1991 par le Conseil régional d'Ile-de-France. Les architectes avaient déjà fait leurs preuves en construisant en 1987 le Lycée du Futur, au sein du Futuroscope de Poitiers. Le lycée Jules-Verne est situé près du parc d'attractions Mirapolis, sur un site triangulaire restreint. Le bâtiment cylindrique inscrit dans la partie principale du triangle contient les salles réservées au personnel, et une série de ponts relient les différents volumes. Un parking de 78 places fait partie intégrante du projet. Avec son profil aérodynamique, le lycée Jules-Verne exprime une confiance dans les formes modernes que les architectes de certains autres pays semblent avoir abandonnée. Malgré ses allures de science-fiction en parfaite harmonie avec son nom, ses concepteurs citent comme source d'influence le TGV (Train à Grande Vitesse français).

Three views of the Lycée Jules Verne give an idea of its dynamic forms, and in particular the sweeping curve which encloses the circular building housing staff facilities.

Drei Ansichten des Lycée Jules Verne vermitteln einen Eindruck seiner dynamischen Formen und insbesondere der geschwungenen Kurve, die das kreisförmige Verwaltungsgebäude umschließt.

Trois vues du Lycée Jules Verne qui donnent une idée de la dynamique de ses formes, comme la courbe impétueuse autour du bâtiment réservé au personnel.

According to the architects, the form of the Lycée Jules Verne was partially inspired by that of the high-speed TGV trains, as the detail below might tend to prove.

Laut Aussage der Architekten diente der französische Hochgeschwindigkeitszug TGV als Inspirationsquelle für das Lycée Jules Verne – wie die Detailansicht unten dokumentiert.

Selon les architectes, et comme le montre le détail ci-dessous, la forme du Lycée Jules Verne a été partielle-ment inspirée par celle du TGV.

Above: An effort has been made to make the entire structure, including its interiors, as bright and cheerful as possible.
Right: The futuristic form of the Lycée Jules Verne is most fully evident in an aerial view, which also shows the proximity of the roads which almost surround the site, in the midst of a "ville nouvelle" development.

Oben: Es wurde große Mühe darauf verwendet, auch in den Innenräumen eine möglichst helle und fröhliche Atmosphäre zu schaffen.
Rechts: Die futuristische Form des Lycée Jules Verne – inmitten einer »ville nouvelle« – kommt am deutlichsten in einer Luftaufnahme zum Ausdruck, die auch zeigt, daß das Gelände nahezu vollständig von Straßen umschlossen ist.

En haut: L'architecte a voulu créer un ensemble et des espaces intérieurs pleins de lumière et de gaieté.
A droite: La forme futuriste du Lycée Jules Verne apparaît de manière évidente sur cette vue aérienne, qui montre aussi la proximité des routes autour du site, au sein de l'extension d'une «ville-nouvelle».

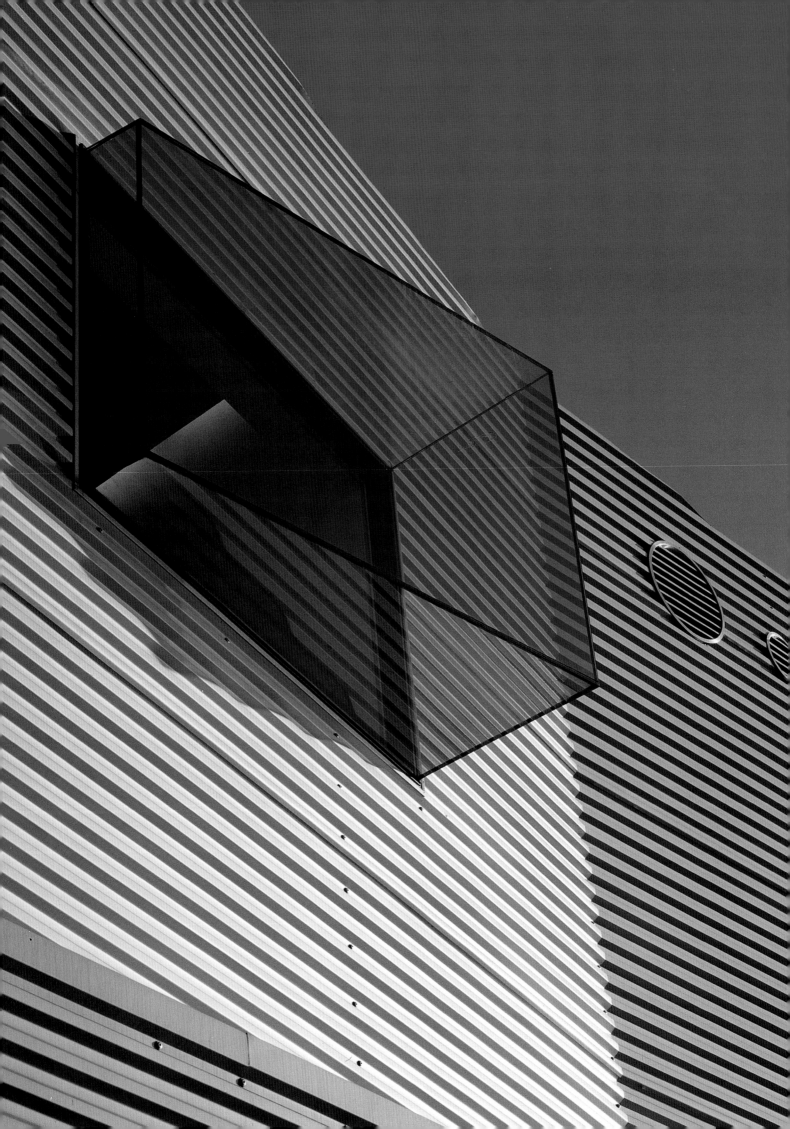

Ben van Berkel

Although not well known outside of architectural circles, Ben van Berkel, born in Utrecht in 1957 will undoubtedly become more famous as a result of his Erasmus Bridge in Rotterdam. Trained at the Architectural Association in London by such figures as Rem Koolhaas and Zaha Hadid, he insists that he is of a different generation, implicitly criticizing them for designing buildings to suit their theories. "If there is a theory," he says "I would apply it in a more tactile, a more physical way, in the sense that one can rethink typologies of organization or the use of materials." Van Berkel has summed up his approach with the term "mobile forces," or the multitude of public, urban, structural and architectural considerations that give form to a project. Fascinated by 1950s engineer | architects like Nervi or Candela, van Berkel worked briefly with Calatrava in the late 1980s. "I like to believe that you can invent as an architect, like a scientist does," says Ben van Berkel. "I like to transgress ideas in order to redefine them."

Der 1957 in Utrecht geborene Ben van Berkel ist bisher nur in Architektenkreisen bekannt – eine Tatsache, die sich mit dem Bau der Erasmusbrug in Rotterdam ändern dürfte. An der Architectural Association in London von Persönlichkeiten wie Rem Koolhaas und Zaha Hadid ausgebildet, besteht van Berkel darauf, einer anderen Generation anzugehören; er wirft seinen Dozenten implizit vor, Bauten nur mit dem Ziel errichtet zu haben, den eigenen Theorien zu genügen. »Wenn überhaupt eine Architekturtheorie existiert«, sagt van Berkel, »würde ich sie auf eine greifbare, physische Art und Weise umsetzen, wobei die Typologien der räumlichen Organisation oder die Verwendung der Materialien neu überdacht werden könnten.« Van Berkel faßt seinen architektonischen Ansatz unter dem Begriff »Mobile Forces« zusammen, worunter er die Vielfalt öffentlicher, urbaner, bautechnischer und architektonischer Erwägungen versteht, die einem Projekt seine bestimmte Form verleihen. Der von den Ingenieuren | Architekten der 50er Jahre wie Nervi oder Candela faszinierte van Berkel arbeitete Ende der 80er Jahre kurz mit Calatrava zusammen. »Ich gebe mich gern der Illusion hin, daß man als Architekt ebenso wie ein Wissenschaftler etwas erfinden kann«, sagt Ben van Berkel. »Ich liebe es, Vorstellungen zu durchbrechen, um sie danach wieder neu zu definieren.«

Bien qu'il ne soit pas encore très connu en dehors des cercles professionnels, Ben van Berkel ne va pas tarder à le devenir grâce à son pont Erasmus réalisé à Rotterdam. Formé à l'Architectural Association à Londres par des célébrités telles que Rem Koolhaas et Zaha Hadid, il tient à faire savoir qu'il appartient à une génération d'architectes différente et reproche implicitement à ses maîtres de construire des bâtiments pour illustrer leurs théories. «En admettant qu'il existe une théorie, dit-il, je l'appliquerais d'une façon plus tactile, plus physique, en repensant les typologies de l'organisation spatiale ou l'utilisation des matériaux.» Van Berkel résume son approche en parlant de «forces mobiles», à savoir la multitude de facteurs publics, urbains, structurels et architecturaux donnant forme à un projet. Fasciné par des ingénieurs | architectes des années 1950 tels que Nervi ou Candela, van Berkel a fait un bref passage par l'agence de Calatrava, à la fin des années 1980. «J'aime à croire que, comme le scientifique, l'architecte peut inventer, dit van Berkel. J'aime transgresser les idées afin de les redéfinir.»

Detail of the Karbouw Office and Workshop, Amersfoort, The Netherlands, 1990–92.

Bürogebäude und Werkstatt der Firma Karbouw, Amersfoort, Niederlande, 1990–92. Detailansicht.

Détail des bureaux et atelier Karbouw, Amersfoort, Pays-Bas, 1990–92.

Karbouw Office and Workshop

Amersfoort, The Netherlands, 1990–1992

Situated in a very ordinary industrial park in Amersfoort, a small city 40 kilometers from Amsterdam, where Ben van Berkel has completed most of his built work, this small, utilitarian building includes a 375 m² workshop on the lower level and 750 m² of offices above. Its long, clean lines are achieved with an external cladding of brickwork and profiled aluminum. One of the most unusual features of the structure is its curved roof. As Ben van Berkel says, "Moving through the internal space, you are constantly aware of this curve, as it changes the ceiling height. Each area gives you the impression of being in a totally different part of the building. This is a particular kind of articulation which results from working on the computer with given geometries. My interest here is in a typology of organization related to the way in which you move through a space, or in the redefinition of the typology. I don't think that we are interested in the esthetic notion of a form, but in its dynamics. Form itself becomes the result of a kind of movement through space."

Der kleine Zweckbau steht in einem ganz alltäglichen Industriegebiet in der Kleinstadt Amersfoort, etwa 40 Kilometer von Amsterdam entfernt, wo Ben van Berkel die meisten seiner Bauwerke realisierte. Der Bau umfaßt einen 375 m² großen Betriebsbereich im Erdgeschoß und 750 m² Bürofläche in den darüberliegenden Geschossen. Das Gebäude verdankt seine langen, klaren Linien der Außenverkleidung aus Klinker und Aluminiumprofilen. Eines der hervorstechendsten Merkmale der Konstruktion ist das gekrümmte Dach. Ben van Berkel bemerkt dazu: »Wenn man sich durch das Innere bewegt, wird man sich ständig der Krümmung bewußt, da sich durch sie die Deckenhöhe verändert. Jeder Bereich erweckt den Eindruck, als befinde man sich in einem völlig anderen Teil des Gebäudes. Es handelt sich um eine besondere Art von Formensprache, die bei der Bearbeitung vorgegebener geometrischer Formen am Computer entsteht. In diesem Zusammenhang bin ich an einer Typologie der räumlichen Organisation interessiert, die in Beziehung zu der Art und Weise steht, in der man sich durch einen Raum bewegt, beziehungsweise an der Neudefinition der Typologie. Meiner Meinung nach interessiert nicht der ästhetische Begriff der Form, sondern vielmehr ihre Dynamik. Die Form selbst wird zum Resultat einer Art von Bewegung durch den Raum.«

Situé dans une zone industrielle très banale d'Amersfoort (petite ville à 40 kilomètres d'Amsterdam) où se trouvent la plupart des ouvrages construits par Ben van Berkel, ce petit bâtiment fonctionnel comprend 375 m² d'atelier au rez-de-chaussée et 750 m² de bureaux à l'étage. Le revêtement extérieur en briques et aluminium profilé lui confère des lignes longues et nettes. Cet édifice se caractérise par son toit arrondi. «Lorsqu'on se déplace à l'intérieur du bâtiment, explique Ben van Berkel, on a tout le temps conscience de cette courbe, car elle fait varier la hauteur du plafond. Chaque zone donne l'impression d'appartenir à une partie totalement différente du bâtiment. Cette sorte d'articulation très particulière résulte du travail sur ordinateur à partir de géométries déterminées. Je m'intéresse ici à une typologie d'organisation liée à la façon dont on se déplace dans un espace, ou plutôt dans la redéfinition de cette typologie. Je ne crois pas que nous nous intéressions à la notion esthétique de la forme, mais à sa dynamique. La forme elle-même devient le résultat d'une sorte de mouvement dans l'espace.»

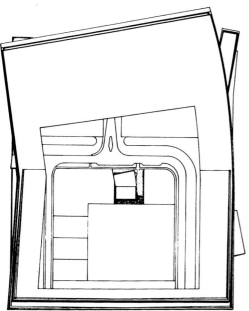

Brick cladding alternates with profiled aluminum surfaces on the exterior, while the entire form of the building is slightly rotated and twisted along lines determined with computer assisted design.

An der Fassade wechseln sich Klinkerverblendung und Profilaluminium-Verkleidung ab, während die Form des Gebäudes mit Hilfe von computergestütztem Entwerfen leicht verschwenkt wurde.

Un revêtement en briques et en aluminium profilé recouvre les surfaces extérieures, tandis que la forme du bâtiment se courbe et s'enroule autour de lignes déterminées par travail sur ordinateur.

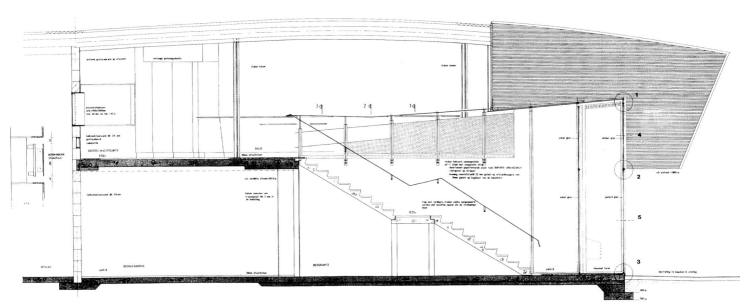

From the side, the building appears to lean forward,
lending it a certain dynamism, which is unusual in such
"industrial park" architecture. The long curve of the
roof gives each interior space a unique aspect despite
the building's relatively small size.

In der Seitenansicht scheint sich das Gebäude nach
vorne zu neigen, wodurch es eine, für eine derartige
»Industriepark«-Architektur recht ungewöhnliche
Dynamik erhält. Die lange Krümmung des Daches
verleiht allen Innenräumen – trotz des relativ geringen
Gebäudeumfangs – eine einzigartige Ausrichtung.

Vu de côté, le bâtiment semble se pencher vers l'avant,
ce qui lui confère un dynamisme rare dans ce type
d'architecture de «zone industrielle». La longue courbe
du toit donne à chaque espace intérieur sa spécificité,
malgré la petite taille du bâtiment.

Erasmus Bridge
Rotterdam, The Netherlands, 1990–1996

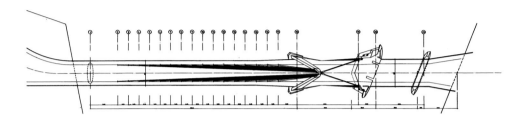

This resolutely asymmetrical bridge, with its inclined 139 meter high pylon giving an impression of delicate equilibrium, connects the center of the city with the Kop van Zuid development area. Because of its situation, at the end of the Boompjes drive which leads most external traffic into the city, the Erasmus Bridge is a highly visible symbol of Rotterdam's modernity. This visibility is accentuated by a carefully studied night lighting of the structure. According to the architect, it is precisely the height of the pylon, and the length of the deck, which has a free span of 284 meters, that determined the unusual angle of inclination of the pylon. As he says, "The conflict between forces and moments in the pylon results in parasitic bending, in which the angle in the uppermost section largely follows the line of moment." Although he was trained as an architect, Ben van Berkel worked briefly in the office of Santiago Calatrava after receiving his diploma at the Architectural Association in London in 1987.

Diese kompromißlos asymmetrisch gestaltete Brücke mit ihrem 139 Meter hohen, geneigten Brückenpfeiler, der den Eindruck eines nicht sehr stabilen Gleichgewichts erweckt, verbindet das Stadtzentrum mit dem Erschließungsgebiet Kop van Zuid. Durch ihre Lage am Ende der Boompjeslaan, über die ein Großteil des Fernverkehrs in die Stadt rollt, bietet die Erasmusbrug ein herausragendes Symbol der Modernität Rotterdams. Ihre Augenfälligkeit wird zusätzlich durch die ausgeklügelte nächtliche Beleuchtung der Baustruktur betont. Dem Architekten zufolge ist der ungewöhnliche Neigungswinkel des Pylons durch dessen Höhe und die Länge der Brückentafel mit einer freien Spannweite von 284 Metern bedingt. Nach seinen Worten »führt der Konflikt zwischen Kräften und Drehmomenten im Pylon zu einer wie durch Störschwingungen bedingten Krümmung, wobei der Winkel im oberen Teilstück hauptsächlich der Linie des Drehmomentes folgt. «Trotz seiner Ausbildung zum Architekten arbeitete Ben van Berkel kurze Zeit im Ingenieurbüro von Santiago Calatrava, nachdem er 1987 sein Diplom an der Architectural Association erhalten hatte.

Avec son pylône incliné de 139 mètres donnant une impression de délicat équilibre, ce pont résolument asymétrique relie le centre de la ville et la zone de développement Kop van Zuid. Situé à l'extrémité de l'avenue Boompjes, principale voie d'accès à la ville, il constitue un symbole particulièrement visible de la modernité de Rotterdam. De nuit, cette visibilité est accentuée par un éclairage soigneusement étudié. L'architecte explique que c'est précisément la hauteur du pylône et la longueur du tablier (portée de 284 mètres) qui ont déterminé l'angle d'inclinaison inhabituel du pylône. Il précise que «le conflit entre les forces et les moments dans le pylône entraîne une flexion parasite dans laquelle l'angle dans la coupe la plus haute suit en grande partie la ligne du moment». Bien qu'architecte de formation, Ben van Berkel a travaillé quelque temps pour la société de Santiago Calatrava après avoir fini ses études à l'Architectural Association de Londres en 1987.

Drawings, a model view, and a night photo of the Erasmus Bridge give an idea of how its form is constituted by a reaction to the forces generated within the pylon, and by the long, thin deck.

Zeichnungen, ein Modell und eine Nachtaufnahme der Erasmusbrug veranschaulichen, wie die Form der Brücke bestimmt wird durch die Reaktion auf die neigungsbedingten Kräfte im Bückenpfeiler und die langgestreckte, dünne Brückentafel.

Dessins de maquette, maquette et photo nocturne du pont Erasmus qui donnent une idée de la constitution de sa forme, réaction aux forces générées par l'inclinaison du pylône et la longueur du tablier.

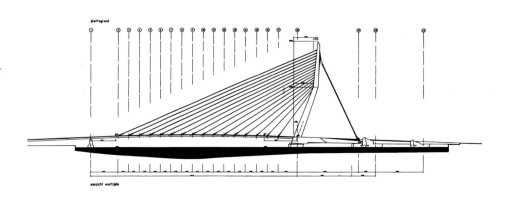

Mario Botta

Born in 1943 in Mendrisio, Switzerland, near the Italian border, Mario Botta designed his first house at the age of 16. Brief contact with Le Corbusier in Paris in 1965, and with Louis Kahn in Venice in 1968 seem to have influenced him, but by the 1970s, he had developed a strong personal style most clearly expressed in the private houses built in Cadenazzo (1970–71), Riva San Vitale (1971–73), or Ligornetto (1975–76). In the 1980s, Botta continued to create powerful geometric designs for houses, often built with brick, but he also began larger scale work, such as his Médiathèque in Villeurbanne (1984–88) or his cultural center in Chambèry (1982–87). With work from Tokyo to California, where the new San Francisco Museum of Modern Art was completed in 1994, Mario Botta has become a figure to be reckoned with on the international architectural scene.

Der 1943 in Mendrisio (Schweiz) geborene Mario Botta entwarf sein erstes Haus im Alter von 16 Jahren. Die kurze Zusammenarbeit mit Le Corbusier in Paris (1965) und Louis Kahn in Venedig (1968) schien ihn zunächst stark zu beeinflussen, aber bereits in den 70er Jahren hatte er einen ausgeprägten persönlichen Stil entwickelt, der in den Privathäusern in Cadenazzo (1970–71), Riva San Vitale (1971–73) und Ligornetto (1975–76) besonders zum Ausdruck kommt. In den 80er Jahren entwarf Botta weiterhin expressive, geometrische, häufig aus Ziegelsteinen errichtete Häuser, aber er widmete sich auch größeren Projekten wie etwa der Médiathèque in Villeurbanne (1984–88) oder dem Kulturzentrum in Chambéry (1982–87). Aufgrund seiner Bauwerke von Tokio bis Kalifornien, wo das neue San Francisco Museum of Modern Art 1994 fertiggestellt wurde, hat sich Botta inzwischen zu einer festen Größe der internationalen Architekturszene entwickelt.

Né en 1943 à Mendrisio (Suisse), à la frontière italienne, Mario Botta a conçu sa première maison à l'âge de 16 ans. Ses brèves rencontres avec Le Corbusier en 1965 à Paris puis avec Louis Kahn en 1968 à Venise semblent l'avoir influencé. Toutefois, dès les années 1970, il avait déjà un style personnel très affirmé, que l'on retrouve nettement exprimé dans les villas construites à Cadenazzo (1970–71), Riva San Vitale (1971–73) et Ligornetto (1975–76). Au cours des années 1980, Botta a continué à concevoir des maisons aux plans géométriques remarquables, souvent construites en briques. Il a aussi entrepris des projets de plus grande dimension comme la médiathèque de Villeurbanne (1984–88) ou le centre culturel de Chambéry (1982–87). En travaillant à Tokyo comme en Californie, où il vient d'achever le nouveau Musée d'art moderne de San Francisco, Mario Botta est devenu une personnalité avec laquelle il faut compter sur la scène internationale.

Evry Cathedral, Evry, France, 1992–95. Above the entrance to the Cathedral, a circular opening and the bell tower.

Cathédrale d'Evry, Evry, Frankreich, 1992–95. Oberhalb des Eingangs zur Kathedrale befinden sich eine kreisförmige Öffnung und der Glockenturm.

La Cathédrale d'Evry, Evry, France, 1992–95. Au-dessus de l'entrée de la cathédrale, une ouverture circulaire et le clocher.

Evry Cathedral

Evry, France, 1992–1995

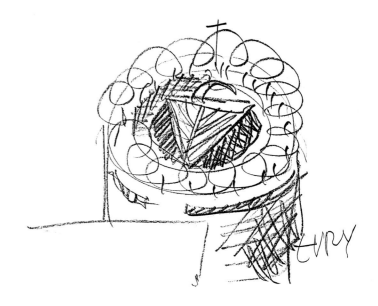

As the most important religious edifice built in France for over a century, the Evry Cathedral, located just to the south of Paris was bound to come under a certain amount of scrutiny. Many criticized the church for spending 60 million French francs at a time when many people are in need, but it was funded with donations. The round structure, inspired by Byzantine-plan churches is 34 meters high and 38.4 meters in diameter. It was built with no fewer than 800,000 bricks made in Toulouse. The interior benches, which seat 800 persons at ground level, and four to five hundred more in upper galleries, are made of Bourgogne oak, and, like the white Carrara marble altar and baptismal font, were designed by the architect. Evry is a new city built without any particular sense of urbanism. Botta's cathedral, which functions as a signal of the city center, visible from the exit of the nearby A6 highway, together with an adjoining housing complex which he also designed, give Evry a certain sense of place.

Seit mehr als einem Jahrhundert ist in Frankreich kein so bedeutender Sakralbau mehr entstanden wie die unmittelbar südlich von Paris gelegene Cathédrale d'Evry. Aus diesem Grunde wurde ihr zwangsläufig ein gewisses Maß an Skepsis zuteil. Man kritisierte die Kirche dafür, 60 Millionen Francs auszugeben, während viele Menschen in Armut leben. Allerdings konnte der Bau aus Spenden finanziert werden. Der runde Baukörper mit einer Höhe von 34 Metern und einem Durchmesser von 38,4 Metern nimmt den Grundriß byzantinischer Kirchen wieder auf; er wurde aus circa 800 000 in Toulouse hergestellten Ziegeln errichtet. Im Inneren finden auf den Bänken im Erdgeschoß 800 Personen Platz sowie weitere vier- bis fünfhundert Gläubige auf verschiedenen Emporen. Das Kirchengestühl besteht aus burgundischem Eichenholz und wurde, ebenso wie der Altar und das Taufbecken aus weißem Carrara-Marmor, vom Architekten selbst entworfen. Evry ist eine junge Stadt, die ohne besonderes städtebauliches Feingefühl entstand. Der Kirchenbau fungiert als Wahrzeichen des Stadtzentrums und ist von der Ausfahrt der nahegelegenen Autobahn A6 zu sehen; zusammen mit einem sich anschließenden, ebenfalls von Botta entworfenen Wohnkomplex verleiht er Evry eine gewisse städtebauliche Prägung.

Il s'agit de l'édifice religieux le plus important construit en France depuis plus d'un siècle. Aussi cette cathédrale située dans la banlieue sud de Paris a-t-elle fait l'objet d'un examen minutieux. Beaucoup l'ont critiquée à cause des 60 millions de francs dépensés à sa construction, à une époque où de nombreuses personnes sont dans le besoin, mais cette somme a été réunie grâce à des donations. Haute de 34 mètres, cette structure ronde de 38,4 mètres de diamètre est inspirée du plan des églises byzantines. Sa construction a nécessité au total 800 000 briques fabriquées à Toulouse. A l'intérieur, les bancs peuvent accueillir 800 personnes au rez-de-chaussée et quatre à cinq cents personnes supplémentaires dans les galeries supérieures. De même que l'autel et les fonts baptismaux en marbre de Carrare, les bancs en chêne de Bourgogne ont été conçus par l'architecte. Evry est une ville nouvelle construite sans réel souci d'urbanisme. Visible depuis la sortie de l'autoroute A6, la cathédrale de Botta signale le centre de la ville. L'ensemble constitué par la cathédrale et le complexe résidentiel contigu, conçu lui aussi par Botta, donne à Evry une certaine personnalité.

Crowned by a ring of trees which might bring to mind the Crown of Thorns, the Cathedral combines anthropomorphic and Byzantine references.

Die Kathedrale wird von einem Ring aus Bäumen gekrönt, der an die Dornenkrone erinnert, und verbindet anthropomorphe Formen mit Anspielungen auf byzantinische Einflüsse.

Surmontée par un ensemble d'arbres qui n'est pas sans évoquer la Couronne d'Epines, la cathédrale associe les références anthropomorphiques et byzantines.

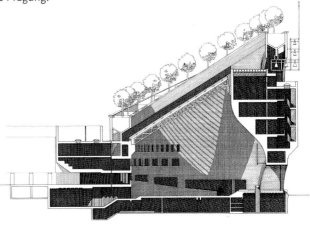

Within the Cathedral, the benches, the altar and baptismal font in white Carrara marble, and the window symbolizing the "tree of life" were all designed by the architect. Niches provide upper level space for parishioners above the main area.

Für das Kirchengestühl, den Altar und das Taufbecken aus weißem Carrara-Marmor sowie das Buntglasfenster, das den »Baum des Lebens« symbolisiert, zeichnete der Architekt höchstpersönlich verantwortlich. Nischen oberhalb des Hauptbereiches bieten zusätzlichen Platz für die Gemeindemitglieder.

A l'intérieur de la cathédrale, les bancs, l'autel et les fonts baptismaux, en marbre de Carrare blanc, ainsi que la baie vitrée symbolisant l' «arbre de vie», ont tous été conçus par l'architecte. A l'étage, une galerie de niches permet aussi d'accueillir les paroissiens.

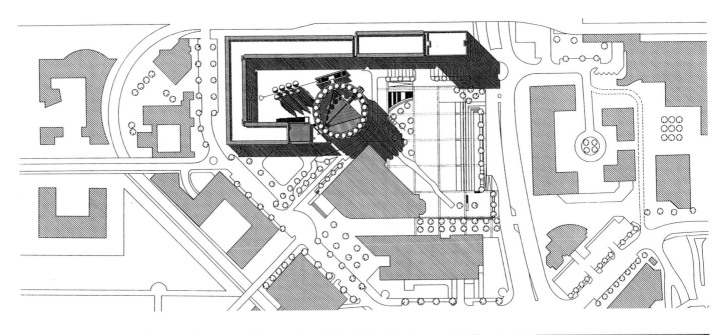

Part of a complex designed by Mario Botta, containing offices and housing, the Cathedral provides Evry with a much needed architectural focal point. A chapel (left) and crypt below the main altar (page 82 bottom) complete the interior spaces.

Als Teil eines ebenfalls von Mario Botta entworfenen Gebäudekomplexes, zu dem Bürogebäude und Wohnhäuser gehören, verleiht die Kathedrale der Stadt Evry endlich das benötigte architektonische Zentrum. Eine Kapelle (links) und eine Krypta unter dem Hauptaltar (Seite 82 unten) vervollständigen die Räumlichkeiten der Kathedrale.

Partie prenante d'un complexe conçu par Mario Botta et comprenant des bureaux et des habitations, la cathédrale a doté Evry d'une personnalité architecturale dont elle avait bien besoin. Une chapelle (à gauche) et une crypte sous l'autel principal (page 82 en bas) ponctuent les espaces intérieurs.

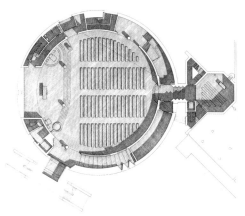

Erick van Egeraat

One of the most promising architects of his generation, Erick van Egeraat was born in 1956 in Amsterdam. He created Mecanoo architects with Henk Döll, Chris de Weijer, Roelf Steenhuis and Francine Houben in Delft in 1983. Their work included large housing projects such as the Herdenkingsplein in Maastricht (1990–92), and smaller scale projects such as their 1990 Boompjes Pavilion, a cantilevered structure overlooking the harbor of Rotterdam, close to the new Erasmus Bridge, or a private house in Rotterdam (1989–91). Signature features of these projects include unexpected use of materials, as in the Rotterdam house where bamboo and steel are placed in juxtaposition with concrete, for example, or an apparent disequilibrium, as in the Boompjes Pavilion. Erick van Egeraat left Mecanoo in 1995 with 17 members of the staff. He has declared his intention to go towards a "warm, inviting architecture", which he calls "Modern Baroque" as opposed to a more neo-modern style favored by Mecanoo.

Der 1956 in Amsterdam geborene Erick van Egeraat gehört zu den vielversprechendsten Architekten seiner Generation. 1983 gründete er zusammen mit Henk Döll, Chris de Weijer, Roelf Steenhuis und Francine Houben in Delft die Gruppe Mecanoo. Zu ihren Arbeiten gehören große Wohnbauprojekte wie der Herdenkingsplein in Maastricht (1990–92) und kleinere Bauten wie der 1990 fertiggestellte Boompjes Paviljoen – eine freitragende Konstruktion in der Nähe der neuen Erasmusbrug, mit Blick über den Hafen von Rotterdam – oder ein Privathaus in Rotterdam (1989–91). Hervorstechende Merkmale dieser Projekte sind die ungewöhnliche Verwendung von Materialien – bei dem Rotterdamer Haus beispielsweise wurden neben Beton auch Bambus und Stahl eingesetzt – oder ein offensichtliches Ungleichgewicht, wie im Falle des Boompjes Paviljoen. 1995 verließ Erick van Egeraat Mecanoo, zusammen mit 17 weiteren Mitarbeitern. Er hat seine Absicht geäußert, eine »warme, einladende« Architektur anzustreben, die er im Gegensatz zu dem eher neomodernen Stil Mecanoos als »Modern Baroque« bezeichnet.

Né en 1956 à Amsterdam, Erick van Egeraat compte parmi les architectes les plus prometteurs de sa génération. Il a créé l'agence Mecanoo avec Henk Döll, Chris de Weijer, Roelf Steenhuis et Francine Houben en 1983 à Delft. Ils ont conçu des cités HLM telles que le Herdenkingsplein à Maastricht (1990–92) et des projets à plus petite échelle comme le Pavillon Boompjes (1990) – une structure en porte-à-faux qui surplombe le port de Rotterdam, près du nouveau pont Erasmus – ou encore une maison individuelle à Rotterdam (1989–91). Ces projets se singularisent par une utilisation originale des matériaux comme par exemple dans la villa de Rotterdam, où le bambou et l'acier côtoient le béton, ou bien par un déséquilibre apparent, comme dans le Pavillon Boompjes. Erick van Egeraat et 17 membres du personnel ont quitté Mecanoo en 1995. L'architecte a exprimé son intention d'évoluer vers «une architecture chaleureuse et accueillante» qu'il qualifie de «baroque moderne» par opposition au style plus néo-moderne privilégié par Mecanoo.

Detail of the "Whale", on the roof of the Nationale Nederlanden and ING Bank, Budapest, Hungary, 1992–94.

Detailansicht des »Wals« auf dem Dach der Nationale Nederlanden and ING Bank, Budapest, Ungarn, 1992–94.

Détail de la «Baleine», sur le toit de la Nationale Nederlanden and ING Bank, Budapest, Hongrie, 1992–94.

Nationale Nederlanden and ING Bank

Budapest, Hungary, 1992–1994

This was a renovation project of a white 1882 Italianate building located on Andrassy ùt, the equivalent in Budapest of the Champs-Elysées, for a large Dutch bank and insurance company. The architects added two floors to the top of the structure, and above all, an organic form which Erick van Egeraat calls the "Whale." As he says, "The Whale is built up of 26 unique laminated timber frames that are hung on the main, steel load-bearing structure which in turn supports two concrete floors. The skin is analogous to shipbuilding, built up of orthogonal battens. On the outside it is finished with zinc and on the inside with linen. The transparent part of the Whale is made of naturally colored curved glass. The form of the skin uses about 103 different glass elements, whereas the glass roof consists of 483 unique glass elements. The laminated glass beams of the roof support the transparent sea of clear glass in which the Whale comfortably floats." He is currently working on an extension to this building.

Das Renovierungsprojekt des weißen Neo-Renaissance Gebäudes aus dem Jahre 1882, das an der Andrassy ùt – dem Budapester Gegenstück zu den Champs Elysées – liegt, erfolgte im Auftrag einer großen niederländischen Bank und einer Versicherungsgesellschaft. Der Architekt stockte den Bau um zwei Geschosse auf und krönte die Konstruktion mit einem organischen Gebilde, das Erick van Egeraat als den »Wal« bezeichnet. »Der Wal setzt sich aus 26 unterschiedlich geformten Schichtholzrahmen zusammen, die an der tragenden Hauptkonstruktion aus Stahl aufgehängt sind, welche ihrerseits zwei Betondecken trägt. Wie die Außenhaut eines Schiffes besteht die Außenwand aus orthogonalen Planken; ihre Außenseite ist mit Zink, die Innenseite mit Leinwand verkleidet. Der transparente Teil des Wals wurde aus naturfarbenem Glas angefertigt. Die Form der Außenhaut besteht aus 103 und das Glasdach aus 483 unterschiedlichen Glasbauelementen. Die aus mehreren Verbundglaslagen konstruierten Dachbalken tragen das transparente Meer aus Glas, auf dem der Wal gemütlich dahintreibt«, beschreibt van Egeraat die Konstruktion; gegenwärtig arbeitet er an einem Anbau für das Gebäude.

Il s'agissait de rénover pour une grande banque néerlandaise un bâtiment blanc de style italien datant de 1882 et situé sur Andrassy ùt, l'équivalent hongrois des Champs-Elysées. Les architectes ont ajouté deux étages au sommet de l'immeuble et, au-dessus, une forme intégrée que Erick van Egeraat appelle la «Baleine». «La Baleine, dit-il, est faite de 26 charpentes en contreplaqué suspendues à la structure porteuse principale, qui est en acier et supporte elle-même deux planchers en béton. La ‹peau› est faite de lattes orthogonales analogues à celles utilisées en construction navale. Elles sont recouvertes de zinc à l'extérieur et d'étoffe à l'intérieur. La partie transparente de la Baleine est faite d'une paroi incurvée en verre coloré naturellement. La forme de la ‹peau› est obtenue grâce à 103 éléments de verre différents, tandis que la verrière est constituée de 483 éléments de verre spécialement conçus pour ce projet. Les poutres en verre feuilleté du toit supportent la mer transparente de verre clair dans laquelle flotte confortablement la Baleine.» Actuellement, van Egeraat travaille sur un projet d'agrandissement de ce bâtiment.

Erick van Egeraat added the two top floors and the "Whale" to this 19th century Italianate structure, taking advantage of a former central courtyard to create a dynamic relationship between traditional and contemporary forms.

Erick van Egeraat fügte dem Neo-Renaissancebau aus dem 19. Jahrhundert zwei weitere Obergeschosse sowie den »Wal« hinzu und nutzte den ehemaligen, zentral gelegenen Innenhof zur Schaffung einer dynamischen Verbindung traditioneller und zeitgenössischer Bauformen.

Erick van Egeraat a ajouté deux étages au sommet, puis cette «Baleine», à une structure à l'italienne du XIX ème siècle. Il a tiré profit d'une ancienne cour centrale et créé une relation dynamique entre des formes traditionnelles et contemporaines.

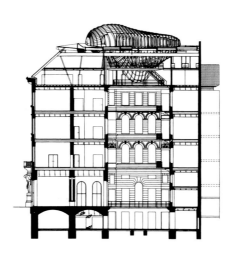

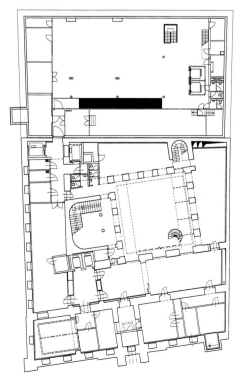

The modernity of the two upper levels designed by the architect creates a transition toward the form of the "Whale" which combines organic and mechanical vocabularies.

Die Modernität der beiden oberen, vom Architekten entworfenen Geschosse erzeugt einen Übergang zum »Wal«, der organische und mechanische Formensprache kombiniert.

La modernité des deux niveaux supérieurs créés par l'architecte permet une transition en direction de la forme de la «Baleine» et l'alliance d'expressions organiques et mécaniques.

Sitting on the roof of the building like an organic extrusion, the "Whale" is unlike almost any other recent piece of architecture, both in its unusual mixture of materials and in its role as a useful extension to an historic monument.

Der auf dem Dach des Gebäudes ruhende, an eine organische Extrusion erinnernde »Wal« unterscheidet sich sowohl aufgrund der ungewöhnlichen Mischung von Materialien als auch in seiner Rolle als sinnvolle Erweiterung eines historischen Gebäudes erheblich von den meisten zeitgenössischen Bauten.

Posée sur le toit du bâtiment, telle une expulsion organique, la «Baleine» ne ressemble à aucune autre création récente, tant par le mélange insolite des matériaux qui la composent, que dans ce rôle de prolongement utile à un bâtiment historique.

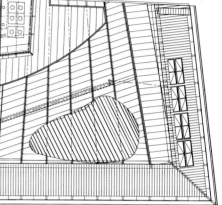

Massimiliano Fuksas

Born in Rome in 1944, Massimiliano Fuksas has been installed for some years in France, although he feels that foreign architects are no longer as welcome there as they were in the 1980s. Working on projects which he usually wins through competitions, such as the new technical high school in Alfortville on the outskirts of Paris, Fuksas conceives of his design in a particularly artistic manner, either through paintings, or small models made of strips of black paper in this case. He maintains that one of the most important changes in recent architecture is that it has become possible to create close links between sculpture and buildings. Indeed, his recent projects, the Niaux grotto cave entrance and Michel de Montaigne University Art School building in Bordeaux, both have a particularly sculptural quality, the first in a more figurative vein, and the second in the tradition of minimalist sculpture.

Der 1944 in Rom geborene Massimiliano Fuksas lebt seit einigen Jahren in Frankreich, obwohl er der Ansicht ist, daß ausländische Architekten dort nicht mehr so gern gesehen sind wie in den 8oer Jahren. Fuksas erhält die Aufträge für seine Projekte, wie die neue Technische Hochschule in Alfortville am Rande von Paris, im allgemeinen durch die Teilnahme an Architekturwettbewerben, und er entwirft seine Bauten auf besonders künstlerische Weise – entweder mit Hilfe von Gemälden oder anhand kleiner Modelle, in diesem Fall aus schwarzen Papierstreifen. Er vertritt die Ansicht, daß eine der bedeutendsten Veränderungen der heutigen Architektur darin besteht, daß enge Verbindungen zwischen Bildhauerei und Architektur möglich geworden sind. Und tatsächlich besitzen seine jüngsten Bauten, der Eingang zur Niaux-Grotte und die Kunstschule der Université Michel de Montaigne in Bordeaux, eine deutlich skulpturale Qualität – ersterer in einem eher metaphorischen Stil, letzterer in der Tradition minimalistischer Plastik.

Né à Rome en 1944, Massimiliano Fuksas est installé en France depuis quelques années, bien qu'il ait le sentiment que les architectes étrangers n'y sont plus aussi bien accueillis que dans les années 1980. Il travaille le plus souvent sur des commandes acquises en remportant des concours, telle que le nouveau lycée technique d'Alfortville, en proche banlieue parisienne. Fuksas conçoit ses plans d'une manière particulièrement artistique, en les peignant ou, dans le cas du lycée cité plus haut, en créant de petites maquettes faites de bandes de papier noir. Il tient à souligner que l'un des changements récents les plus importants qu'ait connu l'architecture consiste dans le fait qu'il est aujourd'hui possible de créer des liens étroits entre la sculpture et les bâtiments. Ainsi, ses dernières réalisations – l'entrée de la grotte de Niaux et l'école des beaux-arts de Bordeaux – ont en commun un caractère particulièrement sculptural, la première dans une veine figurative, tandis que la seconde s'inspire de la tradition sculpturale minimaliste.

Painting by Massimiliano Fuksas representing the Bordeaux Art School, Bordeaux, France, 1993–94.

Gemälde von Massimiliano Fuksas: die Kunstschule der Université Michel de Montaigne in Bordeaux, Frankreich, 1993–94.

Peinture de Massimiliano Fuksas, représentant l'école des beaux-arts de Bordeaux, France, 1993–94.

Entrance to Grotto
Niaux, France, 1988–1993

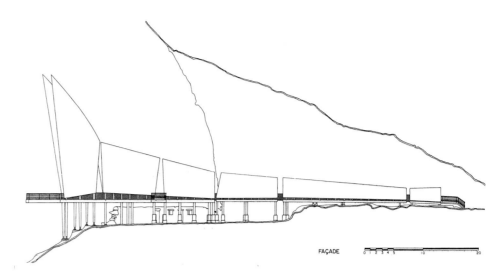

FAÇADE

The Regional Council of the Ariège wanted to create a symbol, testifying to the historical significance of this site which contains cave paintings from the Magdalenian era (11,000 B.C.). The project is intended to create a reception point for the public and a transition from a parking area to the cave entrance. Like some kind of primitive animal rearing its head, or a prehistoric bird about to spread its wings, the entrance designed by Fuksas certainly fulfills the client's desire for a symbol. According to the architect, the cave entrance is meant to resemble an archeological find in itself, which explains the use of pre-rusted Corten steel. It should also be noted that Fuksas feels "that the more contemporary architecture goes forward, the more it resembles sculpture," and Corten steel is, for example, the preferred material of the American sculptor Richard Serra. Fuksas is not, however as interested in American minimalism as some other architects, however, and in Niaux he has created a fascinating link between the prehistoric past and the present.

Der Conseil Régional des französischen Département Ariège wollte hier ein Symbol schaffen, das die historische Bedeutung der Stätte mit ihren Höhlenmalereien aus der Zeit des Magdalénien (11000 v. Chr.) dokumentiert. Im Rahmen des Projektes sollten ein Empfangsbereich für die Besucher sowie ein Übergang vom Parkplatz zum Höhleneingang gestaltet werden. Der von Fuksas entworfene Eingang gleicht einem urzeitlichen Tier, das drohend sein Haupt erhebt, oder einem prähistorischen Vogel, der gerade seine Flügel ausbreiten will, und erfüllt insofern den Wunsch des Auftraggebers nach Symbolik. Laut Fuksas soll auch der Höhleneingang selbst an ein archäologisches Fundstück erinnern, weshalb voroxidierter Corten-Stahl verwendet wurde. Bezeichnenderweise ist Fuksas der Ansicht, daß »die Architektur, je weiter sie sich entwickelt, immer mehr der Bildhauerei ähnelt« – und tatsächlich ist Corten-Stahl das Lieblingsmaterial des amerikanischen Bildhauers Richard Serra. Trotzdem zeigt sich Fuksas nicht so stark an der amerikanischen Minimal Art interessiert wie einige andere Architekten; in Niaux schuf er eine faszinierende Verbindung zwischen prähistorischer Vergangenheit und Gegenwart.

Le Conseil régional de l'Ariège souhaitait créer un symbole pour témoigner de l'importance historique de ce site, qui renferme des peintures rupestres datant du magdalénien (11000 av. J.-C.). Ce projet consiste à créer un point d'accueil pour le public et un espace de transition entre le parking et l'entrée de la grotte. L'entrée créée par Fuksas, qui évoque un animal primitif dressant la tête, ou un oiseau préhistorique prêt à déployer ses ailes, correspond sûrement aux attentes du Conseil régional quant à la symbolique. Selon l'architecte, l'entrée de la grotte elle-même est censée ressembler à une découverte archéologique, ce qui explique qu'il ait utilisé de l'acier corten déjà oxydé. Il faut aussi noter que Fuksas considère que «plus l'architecture contemporaine avance, plus elle ressemble à de la sculpture». Ainsi, l'acier corten est justement le matériau préféré du sculpteur américain Richard Serra. Cependant, Fuksas ne s'intéresse pas autant que certains autres architectes au minimalisme américain et, à Niaux, il a réussit à créer un lien fascinant entre la période préhistorique et notre époque.

Despite having eschewed any attempt at historicist references, Fuksas creates an object whose origins in time are not immediately evident. The rusted appearance of the Corten steel gives the cave entrance a weathered, almost ancient look.

Indem er jeden Versuch historisierender Bezüge vermied, schuf Fuksas ein Objekt, dessen zeitliche Herkunft nicht direkt ersichtlich ist. Die rostige Oberfläche des Corten-Stahls verleiht dem Höhleneingang ein verwittertes, fast schon antikes Erscheinungsbild.

Bien qu'ayant renoncé à toute référence historique, Fuksas crée un objet dont les origines dans le temps n'apparaissent pas immédiatement évidentes. L'aspect rouillé de l'acier corten confère à l'entrée de la grotte une apparence désagrégée, presque antique.

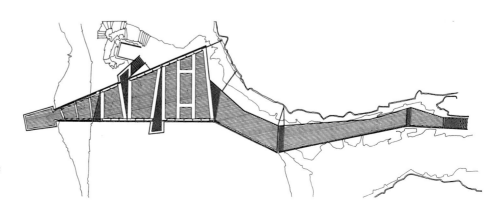

Bordeaux Art School
Bordeaux, France, 1993–1994

The new Arts Center of the Michel de Montaigne University in Bordeaux is intended to bring together different disciplines, such as theater, music sculpture, radio and cinema. The architect calls it "a box full of ideas, an image container." A long, narrow building, cut in half lengthwise and pierced by two large vertical shafts, it is clad in a skin of light green oxidized copper. On the ground floor, the theater space to which the majority of the interior is dedicated, is completely autonomous. The radio studio is positioned on the roof and is clad in wood. Fuksas feels that contemporary architecture is more and more influenced by art. He cites the Italian painter Lucio Fontana as a personal favorite, but it is clear that the sculptural presence of his Bordeaux Art School owes much to sculpture as well. The gathering of different artistic disciplines in this structure obviously pleads in favor of his own belief that architecture itself is now in a position to reclaim its true identity as an art form.

Das neue Zentrum für Kunst der Université Michel de Montaigne in Bordeaux soll unterschiedliche Disziplinen wie Theater, Musik, Bildhauerei, Radio und Film unter einem Dach vereinen. Der Architekt spricht von diesem Bauwerk als einer »Kiste voller Ideen, einem Behälter voller Bilder«. Der lange, schmale Bau ist der Länge nach in zwei Hälften geteilt; er wird von zwei großen vertikalen Säulen durchbohrt und besitzt eine Verkleidung aus hellgrün oxidiertem Kupfer. Der eigenständige Theaterbereich im Erdgeschoß nimmt den größten Teil des Innenraums ein. Das Rundfunkstudio befindet sich auf dem Dach und ist mit Holz verkleidet. Fuksas vertritt die Auffassung, daß die zeitgenössische Architektur in zunehmendem Maß von der Kunst beeinflußt wird. Zwar führt er einen Maler, den Italiener Lucio Fontana, als einen seiner Lieblingskünstler an, doch verdankt die skulpturale Erscheinung der von ihm entworfenen Kunstschule von Bordeaux auch vieles der Bildhauerei. Die Versammlung verschiedener Kunstdisziplinen in diesem Bau bekräftigt erkennbar Fuksas' Überzeugung, daß Architektur in der Lage ist, ihre wahre Identität als Kunstform wieder geltend zu machen.

Le nouveau Centre des arts de l'université Montaigne à Bordeaux est destiné à regrouper différentes disciplines comme l'art dramatique, la musique, la sculpture, la radio et le cinéma. L'architecte en parle comme d'une «boîte pleine d'idées, un conteneur à images». Coupé en deux dans le sens de la longueur et percé de deux grands puits verticaux, ce bâtiment long et étroit est revêtu de cuivre oxydé vert clair. La majeure partie du rez-de-chaussée est occupée par le théâtre, complètement autonome. Le studio de radio, qui est habillé de bois, se trouve sur le toit. Fuksas pense que l'architecture est de plus en plus influencée par l'art. Il cite le peintre italien Lucio Fontana comme son artiste préféré, mais il est clair que son école des beaux-arts de Bordeaux doit également beaucoup à la sculpture. Le regroupement dans un même édifice de différentes disciplines artistiques plaide de toute évidence en faveur de l'idée qu'il défend: l'architecture est aujourd'hui en mesure de retrouver sa véritable identité de genre artistique.

Set in an otherwise banal university environment, the Arts Center stands apart both because of its unusual green color, and because of its apparently blank facades.

Die in die ansonsten banale Universitätslandschaft eingebettete Kunstschule unterscheidet sich von den umliegenden Gebäuden aufgrund ihrer ungewöhnlichen grünen Farbe und ihrer scheinbar undurchbrochenen Fassade.

Situé dans un environnement universitaire plutôt banal, le Centre des arts se distingue non seulement par l'originalité de sa couleur verte, mais aussi par ses façades apparemment aveugles.

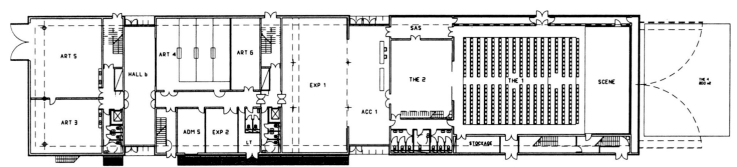

The closed appearance given by the school from the outside gives way to a functional, well-lit interior. Strips of glass and other openings seem to divide the building into segments which float on each other.

Die nach außen geschlossen wirkende Fassade der Kunstschule öffnet sich innen zu funktionalen, lichtdurchfluteten Räumlichkeiten. Glaspaneele und andere Durchbrüche unterteilen das Gebäude in Segmente, die übereinander zu schweben scheinen.

Les façades extérieures sévères de l'école cachent en réalité des espaces intérieurs fonctionnels et largement éclairés. Des panneaux de verre et autres ouvertures semblent diviser le bâtiment en segments flottant les uns sur les autres.

Heikkinen-Komonen

Prior to their Embassy of Finland in Washington, D.C., the first important building built by Mikko Heikkinen and Marrku Komonen, born respectively in 1949 and 1945 in Helsinki, was the Finnish Science Center, Heureka in Helsinki (1988). Indeed, it was this commission which permitted them to form their own partnership after having worked for other architects. They refer to the French writer Paul Valéry to describe their Heureka design. "There are two things that will never cease to threaten the world," Valéry said, "order and disorder." Indeed the building seems to oscillate between a dynamic constructivist asymmetry and a more rational Finnish modernism. A similar dichotomy is shown in the relatively simple geometry of the exterior of their Embassy of Finland, as compared to the complexity of the interior. Heikkinen and Komonen received Finland's Concrete Structure of the Year Award in 1988 and Steel Structure Award in 1989 for the Heureka building. A later work by Heikkinen and Komonen, the European Film School in Ebeltoft, Denmark, (1990–92) shows their capacity to deal with large projects.

Vor ihrem Bau der Finnischen Botschaft in Washington, D.C., hatten Mikko Heikkinen und Marrku Komonen (1949 bzw. 1945 in Helsinki geboren) als erstes größeres Projekt das Finnische Wissenschaftszentrum Heureka in Helsinki (1988) fertiggestellt. Erst dieser Auftrag ermöglichte es ihnen, sich nach jahrelanger Arbeit für andere Architekten auf die Gründung ihres eigenen Büros zu konzentrieren. Bei der Beschreibung ihres Heureka-Entwurfs zitieren sie den französischen Schriftsteller Paul Valéry. »Es gibt zwei Dinge, die nie aufhören werden, die Welt zu bedrohen«, sagte Valéry, »Ordnung und Unordnung.« Und in der Tat scheint das Gebäude zwischen dynamischer konstruktivistischer Asymmetrie und rationaler finnischer Moderne zu oszillieren. Eine ähnliche Dichotomie findet sich auch im Entwurf der Finnischen Botschaft – die relativ einfachen geometrischen Verhältnisse des Außenbaus im Gegensatz zur Komplexität der Innenräume. Für ihr Heureka-Gebäude erhielten Heikkinen und Komonen 1988 den Preis für das beste finnische Betonbauwerk und 1989 den Preis für das beste Stahlbauwerk. Auch ein jüngeres Projekt von Heikkinen und Komonen, die European Film School im dänischen Ebeltoft (1990–92), beweist ihre Fähigkeit im Umgang mit großen Bauprojekten.

Avant l'ambassade de Finlande à Washington, D.C., la première réalisation importante de Mikko Heikkinen et Marrku Komonen (nés en 1949 et respectivement en 1945 à Helsinki) a été Heureka, le Centre finlandais des sciences, à Helsinki (1988). C'est d'ailleurs cette commande qui leur a permis de créer leur propre agence, après une période pendant laquelle ils ont travaillé pour d'autres architectes. Pour décrire leur projet Heureka, ils citent ces propos de Paul Valéry: «Il y a deux choses qui ne cesseront jamais de menacer le monde: l'ordre et le désordre.» De fait, le bâtiment semble osciller entre une asymétrie constructiviste dynamique et un modernisme finlandais plus rationnel. Pour l'ambassade, on note une dichotomie similaire dans la géométrie relativement simple de l'extérieur par rapport à la complexité de l'intérieur. Heikkinen et Komonen ont reçu le prix finlandais de la Construction en béton de l'Année en 1988 et celui de la Construction en acier en 1989 pour le bâtiment Heureka. L'Ecole européenne du cinéma de Ebeltoft (Danemark, 1990–92) a prouvé par la suite que Heikkinen et Komonen étaient aussi capables de mener bien des projets à grande échelle.

Detail of the Embassy of Finland,
Washington, D.C., 1989–94.

Finnische Botschaft, Washington, D.C.,
1989–94. Detailansicht.

Détail de l'ambassade de Finlande,
Washington, D.C., 1989–94.

Embassy of Finland
Washington, D.C., 1989–1994

Located near the Norwegian and Belgian embassies and across from the residence of the Vice President of the United States on Massachusetts Avenue, this structure is set on a steeply sloped small lot which had a number of large trees. One peculiarity of the project is that parking facilities for the staff of 50 had to be created on site, which means that fully one third of the 4,750 m² are set aside for that purpose. The skylit central hall crosses the building's depth longitudinally, providing light for the offices. The steel bridges, ramps and staircases give a complexity which is not expressed on the cubic exterior of the building, clad in moss-green granite, glass tiles, green tinted glass and copper panels. While the desk and fixed furnishings are designed by the architect, the seating ensembles and conference room furnishings are by Charles Eames. Aside from office space and conference rooms, the Embassy also has a small library and a multi-purpose facility called the Finlandia Hall intended for receptions and seminars.

Dieser Bau erhebt sich an der Massachusetts Avenue unweit der Botschaften Norwegens und Belgiens, gleich gegenüber dem Amtssitz des Vizepräsidenten der Vereinigten Staaten, auf einem kleinen, steil abfallenden Grundstück, auf dem früher eine Reihe großer Bäume standen. Eine Besonderheit des Projektes besteht darin, daß auf dem Grundstück Parkgelegenheiten für die 50 Angestellten Platz finden mußten, so daß ein ganzes Drittel der 4750 m² für diesen Zweck bestimmt wurde. Tageslicht fällt in die Mittelhalle ein, die das Gebäude längs in zwei Hälften teilt, und so für Helligkeit in den Büros sorgt. Die stählernen Brücken, Rampen und Treppenaufgänge bewirken eine Komplexität, die dem mit moosgrünem Granit, Glasbausteinen, grün getöntem Glas und Kupferplatten verkleideten Äußeren des Gebäudes nicht anzusehen ist. Während Schreibtische und festinstalliertes Mobiliar von den Architekten entworfen wurden, stammen die Entwürfe für die Sitzgruppen und Möbel der Konferenzräume von Charles Eames. Neben den Büro- und Konferenzräumen verfügt die Botschaft über eine kleine Bibliothek und einen Mehrzwecksaal, die Finlandia Hall, der für Empfänge und Seminare genutzt wird.

Situé sur Massachusetts Avenue, près des ambassades de Norvège et de Belgique et face à la résidence du vice-président des Etats-Unis, ce bâtiment est construit sur un petit terrain en pente raide occupé par de grands arbres. Une des particularités de ce projet résidait dans l'obligation de réserver un tiers des 4750 m² à la création de 50 places de parking pour le personnel. Surmonté d'une verrière, le hall central s'étend sur toute la longueur du bâtiment et permet ainsi d'éclairer les bureaux. Les ponts, les rampes et les escaliers en acier créent une complexité qui n'apparaît pas à l'extérieur de cet édifice cubique recouvert de granit couleur vert mousse, de tuiles en verre et de panneaux mêlant verre teinté vert et cuivre. Les architectes ont conçu le mobilier de bureau et les éléments fixes de décoration, tandis que Charles Eames a conçu les ensembles de sièges et le mobilier des salles de conférence. Outre les bureaux et les salles de conférence, l'ambassade comprend aussi une petite bibliothèque et le Finlandia Hall, espace polyvalent prévu pour les réceptions et les séminaires.

An external trellis, once fully covered by climbing plant will dissimulate the entrance facade behind a green wall, confirming a color-scheme set out by moss-green granite cladding and green-tinted glass.

Entsprechend dem Farbschema, das durch die moosgrüne Granitverkleidung und die grün getönten Glasscheiben bereits festgelegt ist, wird das Spalier vor der Fassade des Gebäudes eines Tages vollständig von Kletterpflanzen überwuchert sein und den Eingangsbereich hinter einer grünen Pflanzenwand verbergen.

Un treillis extérieur, couvert de plantes grimpantes, dissimulera la façade d'entrée derrière un mur vert, confirmant ainsi l'harmonie de couleurs induite par le revêtement en granit vert mousse et le verre teinté de même.

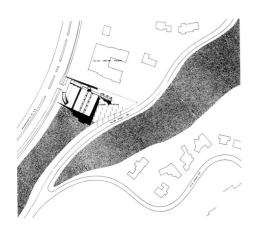

Whereas the exterior facades of the building maintain a relatively strict rectilinear geometry, with the exception of sail-like canopies, the interior spaces offer a selection of angled planes and sweeping curves. A site plan shows the limited area and proximity to roads.

Während die Fassade des Gebäudes – mit Ausnahme der segelartigen Baldachine – eine relativ strenge geometrische Linienführung aufweist, bieten die Innenräume zahlreiche geschwungene Kurven und angeschrägte Ebenen. Der Lageplan zeigt das begrenzte Baugelände und die Nähe zu den umliegenden Straßen.

Alors que les façades extérieures du bâtiment respectent une géométrie rectiligne relativement stricte, à l'exception des auvents en forme de voiles, les espaces intérieurs sont constitués d'angles et d'amples lignes incurvées. Un plan du site met en évidence l'étroitesse du terrain et la proximité des routes.

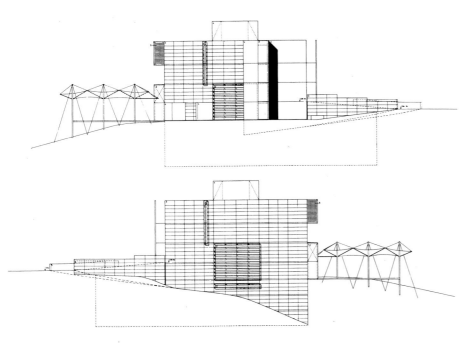

Juha Leiviskä

"The most important building material of the church itself is daylight, which affects the space mainly as indirect reflections, which are at their most intense in the late morning, during morning service," says Juha Leiviskä of his Männistö Church and Parish Center, in Kuopio, Finland. Born in 1936 in Helsinki, he graduated from the Helsinki University of Technology in 1963 and has had his own practice since 1967. Influenced by the geometric forms of the De Stijl movement, Leiviskä's recent work is a testimony both the vitality of Finnish architecture and to the possibilities still left open to modernist design. As the jury citation for the 1995 Carlsberg Award, which he received, indicates, "What sets Leiviskä's work in a class apart is the way in which it is related first to other more rational Finnish masters such as Aulis Blomstedt and, second, and perhaps more significantly, to certain older sources, such as Bavarian Baroque churches and the timber vernacular of Finnish agrarian culture."

»Das wichtigste Baumaterial dieser Kirche ist das Tageslicht. Es beeinflußt den Raum hauptsächlich in Form indirekter Reflexionen, die am späten Morgen, bei der Morgenmesse, besonders intensiv sind«, sagt Juha Leiviskä in der Beschreibung seiner Männisto Kirche und des Gemeindezentrums im finnischen Kuopio. Der 1936 in Helsinki geborene Leiviskä erhielt 1963 sein Diplom an der Technischen Universität Helsinki und gründete 1967 ein eigenes Büro. Seine von der geometrischen Formensprache der De Stijl-Bewegung beeinflußten Bauten zeugen sowohl von der Vitalität der finnischen Architektur als auch von den Möglichkeiten, die modernen Entwürfen immer noch offenstehen. In ihrer Laudatio für den Carlsberg-Preis 1995, den Leiviskä gewann, wies die Jury darauf hin: »Was Leiviskäs Arbeiten einzigartig macht, ist zum einen ihre Beziehung zu anderen, stärker rationalistisch geprägten finnischen Meistern wie etwa Aulis Blomstedt und zum anderen – und dies ist vielleicht von größerer Bedeutung – ihr Bezug zu bestimmten älteren Quellen, wie den Barockkirchen Bayerns und den einheimischen Holzbauten der finnischen Agrarkultur.«

«Dans la construction de cet édifice, le matériau le plus important est la lumière du jour. Elle affecte l'espace essentiellement par un jeu de reflets indirects qui atteignent leur maximum d'intensité en fin de matinée, pendant l'office» explique Juha Leiviskä à propos de l'église et du centre paroissial Männistö de Kuopio (Finlande). Né à Helsinki en 1936, il est diplômé de l'université technologique d'Helsinki (1963) et a ouvert son propre cabinet en 1967. Influencés par les formes géométriques du mouvement De Stijl, ses derniers ouvrages témoignent à la fois de la vitalité de l'architecture finlandaise et des perspectives encore ouvertes au modernisme. En lui décernant le prix Carlsberg en 1995, le jury a déclaré: «Le travail de Leiviskä se singularise d'abord par ses liens avec l'œuvre d'autres maîtres finlandais plus rationnels comme Aulis Blomstedt, et, par ailleurs, avec certaines sources plus anciennes, telles que les églises bavaroises baroques et le bois de construction caractéristique de la culture agraire finlandaise.»

Interior of the Männistö Church, Kuopio, Finland, 1986–92.

Innenansicht der Männistö Kirche, Kuopio, Finnland, 1986–92.

Intérieur de l'église Männistö, Kuopio, Finlande, 1986–92.

Männistö Church and Parish Center

Kuopio, Finland, 1986–1992

It has been said that the design of this 1,620 m² church with 464 seats in the church itself and 140 in the parish hall is derived in its use of light from Aalto, and in its De Stijl-inspired geometry, from Aulis Blomstedt. As Leiviskä himself has said, "My aim has been to achieve a stable spatial organism, formed by the existing environment together with the new building, which in terms of the townscape is based on growth in progressive stages; a fragment of a human-sized town [...] The most important building material of the church itself is daylight, which affects the space mainly as indirect reflections, which are at their most intense in the late morning, during morning service [...] I have tried," continues Leiviskä, "especially to ensure that all the components of the space, such as the different kinds of wall with their works of art, the ceiling, the slanting gallery, the organ, etc., belong together and form an entity. A living interaction of large and small, open and shut, high and low, light and shade, spaces as instruments for light to play on, a continuously changing, shimmering veil of light, these are the characteristics I have aimed at here."

Es wurde behauptet, der Entwurf dieser 1620 m² großen Kirche, mit 464 Plätzen in der Kirche selbst und 140 Plätzen im Gemeindesaal, lehne sich im Umgang mit dem Licht an Aalto und, in seiner De Stijl-inspirierten Geometrie, an Aulis Blomstedt an. Leiviskä selbst hat hierzu einmal gesagt: »Mein Ziel war es, einen stabilen räumlichen Organismus zu erschaffen, der gemeinsam von der vorhandenen Umgebung und dem Neubau gebildet wird und mit Bezug auf das Stadtbild auf fortlaufenden Phase von Wachstum aufbaut; Fragment einer Stadt mit menschlichen Maßstäben [...] Das wichtigste Baumaterial dieser Kirche ist das Tageslicht. Es beeinflußt den Raum hauptsächlich in Form indirekter Reflexionen, die am späten Morgen, bei der Morgenmesse, besonders intensiv sind [...] Vor allem habe ich zu gewährleisten versucht«, fährt Leiviskä fort, »daß sämtliche Raumkomponenten, wie etwa die verschiedenen Wände mit den Kunstwerken, die Decke, die schräge Empore, die Orgel usw., zusammengehören und eine Einheit bilden. Ein lebendiges Zusammenspiel von Groß und Klein, offenen und geschlossenen Formen, Hoch und Tief, Licht und Schatten, Räumen als Instrumenten, auf denen das Licht spielt, ein sich unaufhörlich verändernder, schimmernder Vorhang aus Licht – dies sind die Merkmale, die ich hier verwirklichen wollte.«

On prétend que l'utilisation de la lumière naturelle dans cette église de 1620 m² (464 places assises dans l'église elle-même et 140 dans la salle paroissiale) serait inspirée du travail d'Aalto et que sa géométrie inspirée du mouvement De Stijl serait empruntée à Aulis Blomstedt. Mais Leiviskä lui-même précise: «Mon ambition était de réaliser un organisme spatial stable, formé par la symbiose entre l'environnement existant et le nouveau bâtiment. En termes de paysage urbain, cela suppose une croissance par stades progressifs; un fragment de ville à visage humain [...] Le matériau le plus important est la lumière du jour. Elle affecte l'espace essentiellement par un jeu de reflets indirects qui atteignent leur maximum d'intensité en fin de matinée, pendant l'office [...] J'ai surtout essayé de faire en sorte que tous les composants de l'espace, tels que les différentes sortes de paroi et les œuvres d'art qui les ornent, mais aussi le plafond, les galeries en pente, l'orgue, etc., soient faits pour être ensemble et former une entité. Une interaction entre le grand et le petit, l'ouverture et la fermeture, le haut et le bas, la lumière et l'ombre; des espaces conçus comme des instruments sur lesquels puisse jouer la lumière; un changement permanent; un voile chatoyant de lumière. Voilà les caractéristiques que j'ai souhaité réunir ici.»

Stretched along a long, narrow site, the church (left) and Parish Center (right) create a geometric composition.

Die auf einem langen, schmalen Gelände errichtete Männistö Kirche (links) und das Gemeindezentrum (rechts) bilden eine geometrische Komposition.

L'église (à gauche) et le centre paroissial (à droite) s'organisent en une composition géométrique alignée sur un site long et étroit.

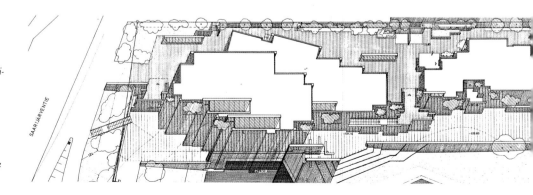

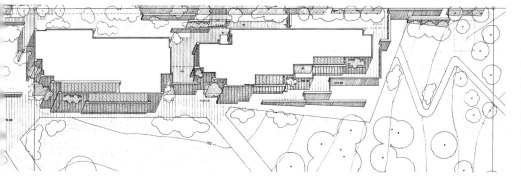

Luminous, soaring spaces, highlighted by the numerous hanging light fixtures show that a rectilinear vocabulary can yield a wealth of spatial volumes.
Pages 112/113: The De Stijl influence is clear in this view of the main facade.

Lichtdurchflutete, emporstrebende Räume, die von zahlreichen Beleuchtungskörpern noch zusätzlich erhellt werden, zeigen, daß eine geradlinige Formensprache eine Fülle dreidimensionaler Raumvolumina erzeugen kann.
Seite 112/113: Ein Blick auf die Fassade macht die Beeinflussung durch De Stijl deutlich.

Des espaces lumineux, élancés et mis en relief par les nombreuses utilisations de la lumière, montrent que même un vocabulaire rectiligne peut produire de riches volumes.
Pages 112/113: Sur cette vue de la façade principale, l'influence de De Stijl apparaît clairement.

Dominique Perrault

Born in 1953, Dominique Perrault was not the most obvious candidate to win the 1989 competition to build a new French national library, to replace the aging facilities located on the rue de Richelieu in Paris. Having defeated the likes of Meier, Koolhaas, Nouvel and Stirling in the competition, Perrault faced a storm of often politically motivated protest against his project, which provided for library stacks placed in four, symmetrical 100 meter high towers, arranged around a 10,782 m² interior garden (size following reductions during the design process) with 250 mature trees. Although the towers were reduced to a height of 80 meters and more books were placed in the base of the structure, the basic plan of Perrault survived this criticism. Inspired by an admiration for minimal art and a critical reflection on modernist tradition, as well as a comparison to castle design, the Bibliothèque de France is likely to remain Dominique Perrault's most important project because of its sheer size, but it will have a lasting impact on thinking about just what it means to be contemporary in architecture.

Der 1953 geborene Dominique Perrault zählte nicht zu den naheliegendsten Kandidaten für den Gewinn des 1989 ausgeschriebenen Architekturwettbewerbs zum Bau der neuen französischen Nationalbibliothek, die die veralteten Einrichtungen an der Rue de Richelieu in Paris ersetzen sollte. Nachdem er Größen wie Meier, Koolhaas, Nouvel und Stirling aus dem Rennen geworfen hatte, schlug Perrault ein – vielfach politisch motivierter – Proteststurm entgegen. Sein Bibliotheksentwurf sah den Bau von vier symmetrischen, 100 m hohen Türmen vor, die rund um einen 10 782 m² großen Garten mit 250 ausgewachsenen Bäumen plaziert werden sollten. Auch wenn man die Türme auf eine Höhe von 80 Metern reduzierte und mehr Bücher im Unterbau des Gebäudes untergebracht wurden, überdauerte Perraults Grundentwurf den Sturm der Kritik. Inspiriert von der Bewunderung für die Minimal Art und der kritischen Reflexion der Moderne wird die an die Tradition des Burgenbaus erinnernde Bibliothèque nationale de France wahrscheinlich schon allein aufgrund ihrer Größe Dominique Perraults bedeutendstes Projekt bleiben. Aber sie wird auch einen nachhaltigen Einfluß auf unsere Vorstellung dessen ausüben, was der Begriff »zeitgenössisch« in der Architektur bedeutet.

Né en 1953, Dominique Perrault ne figurait pas parmi les favoris lors du concours organisé en France en 1989 pour la construction d'une nouvelle bibliothèque nationale destinée à remplacer les bâtiments vieillisants de la rue de Richelieu, à Paris. Après avoir remporté le concours face à des concurrents tels que Meier, Koolhaas, Nouvel et Stirling, Perrault a dû essuyer une véritable tempête de protestations contre son projet – souvent pour des motifs politiques. Ce projet consistait à installer les rayonnages de livres dans quatre tours symétriques de 100 mètres de haut encadrant un jardin intérieur de 10 782 m² (chiffre définitif) planté de 250 arbres adultes. La hauteur des tours a été ramenée à 80 mètres et il est prévu qu'un nombre plus important de livres trouve place à la base de l'édifice, mais le plan général de Perrault a toutefois survécu au tollé qui l'a accueilli. La Bibliothèque nationale de France témoigne de l'admiration de l'architecte pour l'art minimal et d'une réflexion critique sur la tradition moderniste, en même temps qu'elle évoque l'architecture des châteaux. Ce projet demeurera probablement, par sa taille, la plus importante réalisation de Dominique Perrault, et elle aura sans doute un impact durable sur la réflexion menée à propos de la contemporanéité en architecture.

Detail of the facade of one tower of the Bibliothèque nationale de France, Paris, France, 1989–96.

Fassadendetail eines Turmes der Bibliothèque nationale de France, Paris, Frankreich, 1989–96.

Détail de la façade de la Bibliothèque nationale de France, Paris, 1989–96.

Bibliothèque nationale de France
Paris, France, 1989–1996

In terms of sheer size and cost, this is the most ambitious of the Grands Travaux launched by President François Mitterrand. Its construction cost of 3.6 billion French francs (taxes not included) works out to a relatively modest 9,859 French francs per square meter, but the total budget, including computer facilities is over 7.2 billion francs. Its four angle towers are each 80 meters tall, some 20 meters less than the architect had hoped. The seven hectare lot is located on the banks of the Seine in a difficult urban context dominated until recently by the rail yards of the Austerlitz Station. 12 million books will be housed here, and some 3,500 places offered to readers. At the level of the internal garden, below grade, the reading rooms are no less than 13 meters high, giving a feeling of space which is not typical of modernist architecture. According to Perrault, the central, wooded garden is a symbolic allusion to the Garden of Eden, source of sin, and knowledge. He also maintains that because this garden is dug deep into the earth the whole structure differs radically from modernist designs which rarely disturbed the surface of their sites.

Was Größe und Baukosten betrifft, handelt es sich um das ehrgeizigste Projekt unter den von Präsident François Mitterand initiierten Grands Travaux. Aus den Baukosten von 3,6 Billionen Francs (zuzüglich Steuern) ergibt sich ein relativ moderater Baupreis von 9859 Francs pro Quadratmeter; die Gesamtkosten einschließlich der Computerinstallationen belaufen sich allerdings auf über 7,2 Billionen Francs. Jeder der vier abgewinkelten Türme ist 80 Meter hoch, also etwa 20 Meter weniger, als vom Architekten gewünscht. Die sieben Hektar große Baufläche liegt am Ufer der Seine in einem schwierigen städtebaulichen Kontext, der noch bis vor kurzem von den Gleisanlagen des Bahnhofs Gare d'Austerlitz bestimmt wurde. Hier sollen 12 Millionen Bücher Platz finden und etwa 3500 Leseplätze entstehen. Die Deckenhöhe der Lesesäle auf dem Niveau des Innengartens unter Planum beträgt ganze 13 Meter und vermittelt ein für moderne Architektur untypisches Raumgefühl. Nach eigenen Worten spielt Perrault mit dem baumbestandenen Innengarten symbolisch auf den Garten Eden an, den Ursprung der Sünde und des Wissens. Seiner Meinung nach unterscheidet sich der gesamte Bau auch insofern radikal von Entwürfen der Moderne – die selten die Oberfläche ihrer Standorte tief aufwühlen –, als der Garten tief in die Erde versenkt ist.

Par sa taille et son coût, il s'agit là du plus ambitieux des Grands Travaux lancés par le président François Mitterrand. Sa construction a coûté 3,6 milliards de francs (hors T.V.A.), soit une somme relativement modeste de 9859 francs par mètre carré. Cependant, en comptant l'ensemble des équipements informatiques, le budget total s'élève à plus de 7,2 milliards. Les quatre tours en angle font 80 mètres de haut, soit 20 mètres de moins que la hauteur initialement prévue par l'architecte. Le terrain de 7 hectares se situe au bord de la Seine dans un contexte urbain difficile, occupé jusqu'ici en grande partie par les voies de dépôt de la gare d'Austerlitz. Le bâtiment renfermera 12 millions de livres et quelque 3500 places réservées aux lecteurs. Au niveau du jardin intérieur, c'est-à-dire au-dessous du niveau du rez-de-chaussée, les salles de lecture offrent 13 mètres sous plafond, ce qui donne une impression d'espace inhabituelle dans l'architecture moderne. D'après Perrault, le jardin central et boisé est une allusion au Jardin d'Eden, source du péché et de la connaissance. Il soutient aussi que, par son jardin enfoncé profondément au-dessous du niveau des bâtiments, l'ensemble se distingue radicalement des réalisations modernistes, qui ont rarement dérangé la surface de leur site.

Set in an industrial zone on the periphery of Paris (13th arrondissement), along the banks of the Seine, the four towers of the library enclose a vast wooded area which the architects compares to the Garden of Eden.

Die in einem Industriegebiet am Stadtrand von Paris (13. Arrondissement), am Ufer der Seine, gelegenen vier Türme der Bibliothek umschließen eine große baumbestandene Fläche, die der Architekt mit dem Garten Eden vergleicht.

La bibliothèque occupe un ancien site industriel du XIIIᵉ arrondissement de Paris, le long des berges de la Seine. Ses quatre tours encadrent un grand jardin boisé que l'architecte compare au Jardin d'Eden.

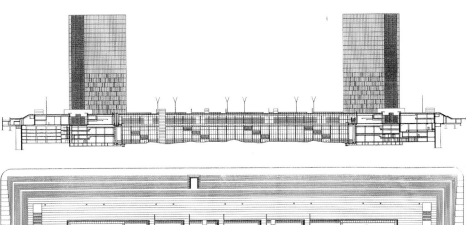

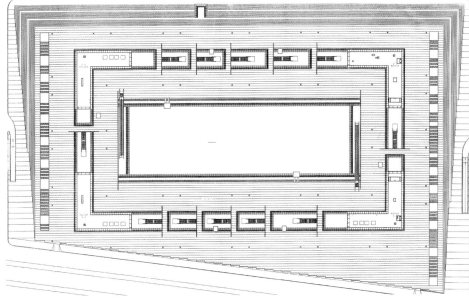

Like four open books, the 80 meter high towers enclose
the rectangular garden which is planted well below
grade. The minimalist penchant of the architect is
obvious in the geometric facade design of the towers.

Wie vier aufgeschlagene Bücher umschließen die
80 Meter hohen Türme den rechtwinkligen, tiefer-
gelegten Garten. Die Vorliebe des Architekten für
Minimal Art zeigt sich im geometrischen Fassaden-
design der Türme.

Telles quatre livres ouverts, les tours de 80 mètres
délimitent le jardin rectangulaire, profondément
enfoncé en contrebas. Les goûts minimalistes de
l'architecte apparaissent de manière évidente dans
la façade géométrique de ses tours.

Inaccessible to the public, the garden faces the level
of the main reading rooms which are reserved for
researchers. Even the view of the garden is obscured
from the public deck above, by railings which
extend horizontally.

*Der für den Publikumsverkehr nicht zugängliche
Garten liegt auf einer Ebene mit den Hauptlesesälen,
die Wissenschaftlern vorbehalten sind. Selbst der Blick
auf den Garten von der öffentlich begehbaren Freifläche
oberhalb der Lesesäle wird durch horizontal verlaufende
Brüstungen verdeckt.*

*Inaccessible au public, le jardin est situé au niveau des
principales salles de lecture, réservées aux chercheurs.
La vue du jardin est même cachée au public par des
rampes horizontales.*

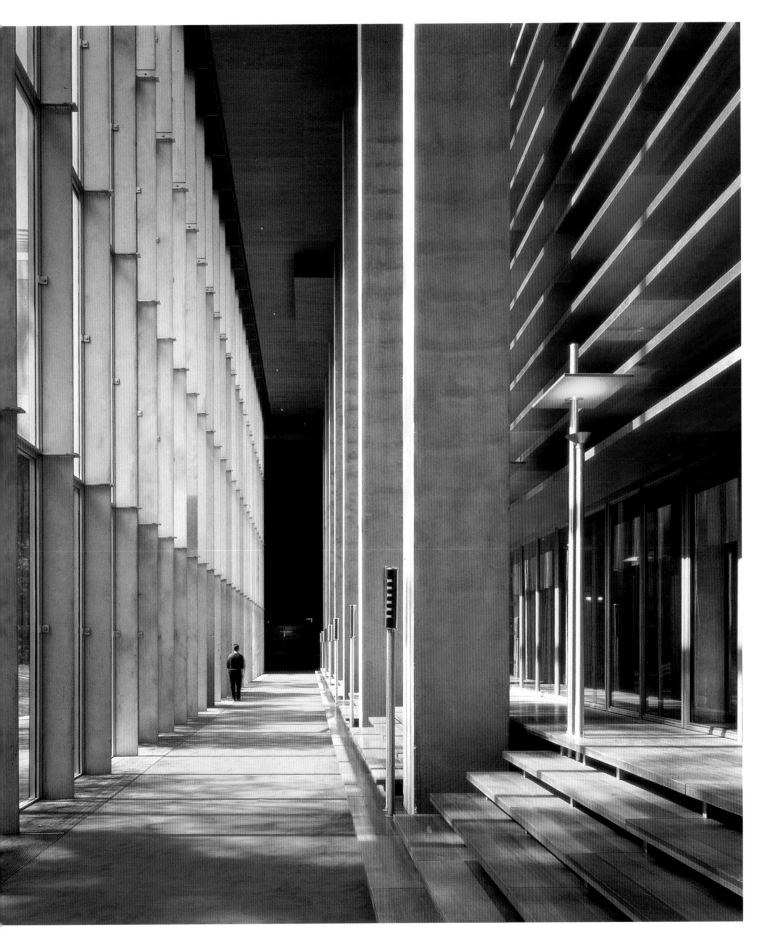

The metallic harshness of much of the library is
attenuated by the use of red carpets and wooden
panels. An unusual stainless steel "chain-mail"
is used on ceilings and on some walls.

Das metallisch-harte Erscheinungsbild großer Teile der
Bibliothek wird durch die Verwendung roter Teppiche
und Holzpaneele gemildert. Ein ungewöhnlicher,
rostfreier »Kettenpanzer« aus Edelstahl ziert die
Decken und einige Wände.

L'effet métallique est atténué par l'utilisation de
moquettes rouges et de lambris. Une surprenante
«cotte de mailles» en acier recouvre les plafonds et
certains murs.

Richard Rogers

"We were young and we wanted to shock them." This is how Renzo Piano recently described the design of the Centre Georges Pompidou (1971–77) which he worked on with Richard Rogers. This goal was attained. Piano and Rogers both joined the ranks of the most famous architects in the world, known for a "High-Tech" style which Rogers affirmed with very visible structures like the Lloyd's of London headquarters (1978–86). In recent years Rogers has refined his visually complex assemblages in buildings like the Channel 4 television headquarters in London (1990–94), and his Law Courts in Bordeaux promise for the first time to enclose and conceal parts of the structure in large pods. Richard Rogers has also participated in large-scale urban schemes like the Lu Jia Zui Masterplan (Shanghai, China, 1992–), a new business area of 4 square kilometers for the Chinese city. In a series of lectures delivered in London in 1995, Richard Rogers placed an emphasis on the responsibility of architects in urban development and toward the environment.

»Wir waren jung, und wir wollten schockieren.« Mit diesen Worten beschrieb Renzo Piano vor kurzem den Entwurf des Centre Georges Pompidou (1971–77), den er zusammen mit Richard Rogers erarbeitete. Dieses Ziel wurde erreicht. Sowohl Piano als auch Rogers stiegen auf in die Gruppe der berühmtesten Architekten der Welt. Sie wurden bekannt für ihren »High-Tech«-Stil, den Rogers mit vielbesprochenen Bauten wie dem Bürokomplex von Lloyd's of London (1978–86) bestätigte. In den letzten Jahren verfeinerte Rogers seine visuell komplexen Assemblagen in Bauwerken wie dem Channel 4 Television Headquarters in London (1990–94), und seine Gerichtsgebäude in Bordeaux versprechen zum ersten Mal, Teile ihrer Struktur in großen Hülsen einzukapseln und zu verbergen. Daneben beteiligte sich Richard Rogers an Stadtplanungen in großem Maßstab wie im Falle des Lu Jia Zui-Bebauungsplans (Shanghai, China, 1992–), bei dem ein neues Geschäftsviertel von 4 Quadratkilometern Größe für diese chinesische Stadt angelegt werden soll. In einer Reihe von Vorträgen, die er 1995 in London hielt, betonte Rogers die Verantwortung der Architekten auf dem Gebiet der Stadtplanung und der Umwelt gegenüber.

«Nous étions jeunes et nous voulions les choquer.» Voilà comment Renzo Piano évoquait récemment la création du Centre Georges Pompidou (1971–77), qu'il a conçu en collaboration avec Richard Rogers. En atteignant leur objectif, Piano et Rogers ont alors rejoint le cercle des architectes les plus célèbres du monde. Leur notoriété est due au style «high-tech» que Rogers a ensuite confirmé avec des édifices très ostensibles tels que le siège social de la Lloyd's à Londres (1978–86). Ces dernières années, Rogers a peaufiné ses assemblages visuels complexes pour créer des bâtiments tels que le siège social de la chaîne Channel 4, à Londres (1990–94) et le palais de justice de Bordeaux, où il promettait d'innover en enfermant des parties de la structure dans de grands modules. Richard Rogers a aussi participé à l'élaboration de plans urbanistiques à grande échelle comme celui de Lu Jia Zui (Shanghaï, Chine, 1992–), nouveau quartier d'affaires de 4 kilomètres carrés. Lors d'une série de conférences données à Londres en 1995, Richard Rogers a mis l'accent sur la responsabilité des architectes dans le développement urbain et à l'égard de l'environnement.

Richard Rogers, European Court of Human Rights, Strasbourg, France, 1989–95. View taken from below the stairway in the entrance area.

Richard Rogers, Europäischer Gerichtshof für Menschenrechte, Straßburg, Frankreich, 1989–95. Ansicht des Treppenhauses vom Eingangsbereich aus.

Richard Rogers, Cour européenne des droits de l'homme, Strasbourg, France, 1989–95. Vue du bas de l'escalier, dans l'entrée.

European Court of Human Rights
Strasbourg, France, 1989–1995

Richard Rogers was chosen to build this project on September 19, 1989, as a result of a competition organized by the city of Strasbourg. Rogers proposed a curved, double-headed building, corresponding to the bi-partite function of the organization. When Rogers was chosen, the 240 million French franc construction cost corresponded to facilities for 25 member states, but with the fall of the Berlin Wall, that number increased to 34, and 3,000 m² of new office space were added to the project in the spring of 1992. The final cost increased to 455 million French francs by December 1994. The final project, a 28,000 m² structure, includes 860 m² for the main court room, 520 m² for the meeting room of the Commission, 4,500 m² of meeting rooms, and 16,500 m² for the offices, laid out in two, curved, seven-story structures which follow the curve of the Ill River. It should be noted that the so-called "Protocol 11" signed by all of the member states since May 11, 1994 and already ratified by nine of them, provides that the current bi-partite organization will be dissolved in favor of a unique court structure. Through no fault of his own, the very symbolism of Richard Rogers's building thus no longer corresponds to the actual organization of the European Court of Human Rights.

Im Rahmen eines von der Stadt Straßburg ausgeschriebenen Wettbewerbs wurde Richard Rogers am 19. September 1989 für den Bau dieses Projekts ausgewählt. Rogers hatte einen geschwungenen, doppelköpfigen, der zweigliedrigen Funktionsweise der Organisation entsprechenden Entwurf eingereicht. Als man sich für Rogers entschied, sollte das auf 240 Millionen Francs veranschlagte Vorhaben Raum für 25 Mitgliedstaaten bieten. Mit dem Fall der Berliner Mauer erhöhte sich deren Zahl jedoch auf 34, so daß das Projekt im Frühjahr 1992 um 3000 m² neue Büroflächen erweitert wurde. Schließlich wuchsen die Gesamtkosten bis zum Dezember 1994 auf 455 Millionen Francs an. Das Projekt umfaßt in seiner endgültigen Form 28 000 m², davon 860 m² für den großen Gerichtssaal, 520 m² für den Sitzungssaal der Kommission, 4500 m² für die übrigen Konferenzräume und 16 500 m² für die Büros. Die Räume sind in zwei geschwungenen, siebengeschossigen Baukörpern untergebracht, die einer Biegung der Ill folgen. Ironischerweise sieht das seit dem 11. Mai 1994 von allen Mitgliedstaaten unterzeichnete und bereits von neun Mitgliedstaaten ratifizierte 11. Zusatzprotokoll vor, die zweigliedrige Struktur des Gerichts durch eine einheitliche Gerichtsorganisation abzulösen. Die von Rogers eigens für dieses Bauwerk entwickelte Symbolik entspricht somit nicht mehr der gegenwärtigen Organisationsform des Europäischen Gerichtshofs für Menschenrechte, wenngleich der Architekt hierfür nicht verantwortlich zu machen ist.

Le projet de Richard Rogers a été sélectionné le 19 septembre 1989 à la suite d'un concours organisé par la ville de Strasbourg. Rogers proposait de construire un édifice arrondi et bicéphale reflétant la nature bipartite de l'organisation. Le coût de construction estimé à 240 millions de francs correspondait à une installation conçue pour 25 Etats membres. Mais, avec la chute du mur de Berlin, ce nombre est passé à 34. Au cours du printemps 1992, 3000 m² de bureaux supplémentaires ont dû être ajoutés au projet. En décembre 1994, le coût total s'élevait à 455 millions de francs. Le projet final prévoyait un édifice de 28 000 m², dont 860 m² consacrés à la salle d'audience, 520 m² à la salle de réunion de la Commission, 4500 m² aux différentes salles de réunion, et 16 500 m² aux bureaux. Cette structure devait être constituée de deux bâtiments de sept étages dont la façade épousait la courbe de la rivière Ill. Il faut noter que le «Protocole 11», signé par tous les Etats membres depuis le 11 mai 1994 et déjà ratifié par neuf d'entre eux, précise que l'organisation aujourd'hui tripartite sera dissoute au profit d'une structure comportant une seule cour. Ainsi, sans que Richard Rogers puisse en être tenu pour responsable, le symbolisme même de son projet ne correspond plus à l'organisation réelle de la Cour européenne des droits de l'homme.

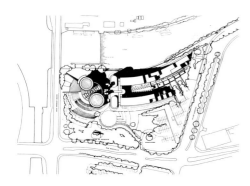

Site plan showing relationship between building and the Ill River.

Der Lageplan zeigt das Verhältnis zwischen dem Gebäude und der Ill.

Plan du site montrant la relation entre le bâtiment et la rivière Ill.

The entrance rotunda and a view of the complex on the Ill River, showing the curving office wings.

Die Rotunde am Eingangsbereich sowie eine Ansicht des gesamten Gebäudes am Ufer der Ill verdeutlichen die geschwungene Linienführung der Bürobereiche.

Rotonde d'entrée et vue du complexe qui domine la rivière et met en évidence la courbe de ses ailes bureaux.

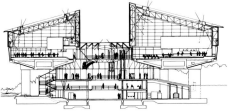

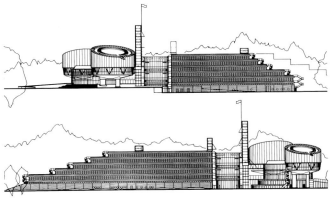

Left: *A view of the entrance area, also visible at the center of the section above.* **Above:** *A view of the court chamber and two elevations, showing the office wings trailing the "head" of the structure.*

Links: *Ansicht des Eingangsbereichs, der auch im Zentrum des Querschnittes (S. 129 oben) zu sehen ist.* **Oben:** *Der Gerichtssaal sowie zwei Aufrisse, die zeigen, wie sich die Büroflügel an den »Kopf« des Komplexes anlagern.*

A gauche: *L'entrée, également visible au centre de la section ci-dessus.* **Ci-dessus:** *Une image de la cour de justice et deux élévations, montrant les ailes bureaux qui soulignent le «cerveau» de la structure.*

Aldo Rossi

Aldo Rossi, born in 1931 in Milan is one of the outstanding figures of modern Italian architecture, as the attribution of the Pritzker Prize to him in 1990 attests. Undoubtedly influenced by a painter like Giorgio de Chirico, he also aspires to the curious kind of neoclassical grandeur imagined by Claude-Nicolas Ledoux. He has often written of his view of the city as a collection of "urban facts" or specific objects related to a given time and place. Although much of his work can appear austere in images, there is a play of light and space over and around the materials which he chooses, whether they might be relatively inexpensive or luxurious, as in the 1989 Il Palazzo Hotel in Fukuoka, Japan, which gives his architecture an undeniable presence and identity. Though rather harsh and industrial in appearance, the Bonnefanten Museum fits in well with the historical context of its location, including the neighboring Wiebengahal, and exhibits art efficiently.

Der 1931 in Mailand geborene Aldo Rossi zählt zu den herausragenden Größen der modernen italienischen Architektur, wie die Verleihung des Pritzker Preises 1990 bestätigt. Ohne Zweifel beeinflußt von Malern wie Giorgio de Chirico, strebt er in seinen Bauten eine eigenwillige Art neoklassizistischer Erhabenheit an, die an die Bauwerke von Claude-Nicolas Ledoux erinnert. Rossi schrieb häufig über seine Auffassung von der Stadt als einer Ansammlung »urbaner Tatsachen« oder spezifischer Objekte, die mit bestimmten Orten und Zeiten in Beziehung stehen. Obwohl ein Großteil seiner Arbeiten auf Bildern äußerst nüchtern wirken kann, ergibt die Wahl seiner Materialien – ob relativ preiswert oder luxuriös, wie im Falle des 1989 erstellten Il Palazzo Hotel im japanischen Fukuoka – ein Spiel von Licht und Raum, das Rossis Architektur eine unbestreitbare Präsenz und Identität verleiht. Trotz seines eher schroffen, an eine Fabrik erinnernden Erscheinungsbildes fügt sich das Bonnefanten Museum gut in den historischen Kontext seiner Umgebung ein, zu der auch die benachbarte Wiebengahal zählt, und bietet einen passenden Rahmen für die Ausstellung von Kunst.

Né en 1931 à Milan, Aldo Rossi est une des figures les plus remarquables de l'architecture moderne italienne. Le prix Pritzker lui a d'ailleurs été attribué en 1990. Nettement influencé par le peintre Giorgio de Chirico, il aspire aussi au curieux genre de grandeur néoclassique imaginé par Claude-Nicolas Ledoux. Il a souvent décrit sa vision de la ville comme une collection de «faits urbains» ou d'objets spécifiques liés à un temps et à un lieu donnés. Même si une grande partie des concepts à la base de son travail peuvent paraître austères, il se crée sur et autour des matériaux qu'il choisit (qu'ils soient relativement bon marché ou luxueux, comme dans le Palazzo Hotel de Fukuoka construit au Japon en 1989) un jeu entre lumière et espace qui donne à son architecture une présence et une identité indéniables. Bien que d'aspect assez sévère et industriel, le musée Bonnefanten s'insère parfaitement dans le contexte historique du lieu qu'il occupe (y compris le Wiebengahal voisin) et réussit à mettre efficacement en valeur les objets d'art qu'il abrite.

Aldo Rossi, Bonnefanten Museum, Maastricht, The Netherlands, 1990–94. Detail of the zinc-covered dome.

Aldo Rossi, Bonnefanten Museum, Maastricht, Niederlande, 1990–94. Detail der zinkverkleideten Kuppel.

Aldo Rossi, Musée Bonnefanten, Maastricht, Pays-Bas, 1990–94. Détail du dôme couvert de zinc.

Bonnefanten Museum

Maastricht, The Netherlands, 1990–1994

Part of a reconstruction program of the "Ceramique" district of Maastricht, located across the Maas River from the city center, the new Bonnefanten Museum offers an area of 6,000 m² to which 3000 m² in the newly restored Wiebengahal have been added. The Wiebengahal was the first reinforced concrete building erected in The Netherlands in 1912. Its industrial vocabulary certainly gave Aldo Rossi the point of departure for this 40 million florin museum, clad in Dutch brick and Irish limestone. The interior is very straightforward, with rough Malaysian timber board floors. The museum houses a varied collection ranging from local archeology to very contemporary art. The most unusual feature of the E-shaped plan is a 28 meter high, domed structure. In an article written in 1991, Rossi noted that the "grandiosity" of the zinc-clad dome was motivated by "its link with the purest architectural tradition from the Classical world to Turin's Alessandro Antonelli." This said, the cylindrical volume also looks very much like tea pots designed by Rossi.

Als Teil des Sanierungsprogramms für das »Ceramiqueterrein« in Maastricht, das gleich gegenüber dem Stadtzentrum auf dem anderen Maasufer liegt, bietet das neue Bonnefanten Museum eine Fläche von 6000 m², zu der weitere 3000 m² in der neu renovierten Wiebengahal hinzukommen. Diese 1912 erbaute Halle war das erste Stahlbetonbauwerk der Niederlande, und ihre industrielle Formensprache gab den Anstoß zu Aldo Rossis 40 Millionen Gulden teurem Museumsbau, der mit niederländischen Ziegeln und irischem Kalkstein verkleidet ist. Die Innenausstattung mit ihrem rauhen Dielenboden aus malaysischem Holz ist relativ einfach gehalten. Das Museum beherbergt eine vielfältige Sammlung, angefangen bei archäologischen Funden aus der Umgebung bis hin zu modernster Kunst. Das ungewöhnlichste Detail des E-förmig angelegten Gebäudes ist eine 28 Meter hohe, mit einer Kuppel gekrönte Konstruktion. In einem Artikel von 1991 schreibt Rossi, die »Großartigkeit« der zinkverkleideten Kuppel beruhe auf »ihrer Verbindung mit reinster architektonischer Tradition, die sich von der Welt der Antike in das Turin Alessandro Antonellis fortsetzt«. In Anbetracht dieser Worte sieht denn auch der zylindrische Baukörper den von Rossi entworfenen Teekannen recht ähnlich.

Le musée Bonnefanten fait partie d'un programme de reconstruction du quartier «Ceramique» de Maastricht, situé face au centre-ville, sur l'autre rive de la Meuse. Il offre une surface de 6000 m² auxquels viennent s'ajouter les 3000 m² du Wiebengahal récemment restauré. Ce dernier est le premier bâtiment en béton armé construit aux Pays-Bas (1912). Son vocabulaire industriel a certainement donné à Aldo Rossi le point de départ de son musée revêtu de briques hollandaises et de calcaire irlandais, qui a coûté 40 millions de florins. Le plancher en bois brut de Malaisie donne à l'intérieur un aspect très sobre. Ce musée renferme une collection variée qui compte des découvertes archéologiques locales comme des œuvres d'art très contemporain. L'édifice en forme de E se singularise par la présence d'un dôme haut de 28 mètres. Dans un article écrit en 1991, Rossi note que le caractère grandiose de ce dôme recouvert de zinc se justifiait en raison de «son lien avec la plus pure tradition architecturale, de l'Antiquité gréco-latine à Alessandro Antonelli, de Turin». Cela dit, le volume cylindrique n'est pas sans rappeler les théières dessinées par Rossi.

Page 133 bottom: A 1992 drawing by the architect showing the dome area.
Page 133 top: The museum as it is seen from across the Maas River.

Seite 133 unten: Eine Zeichnung des Architekten aus dem Jahre 1992, die den Kuppelbereich zeigt.
Seite 133 oben: Ansicht des Museums vom gegenüberliegenden Maasufer.

Page 133 en bas: Dessin de l'architecte, datant de 1992, le dôme.
Page 133 en haut: Le musée, vu de l'autre côté de la Meuse.

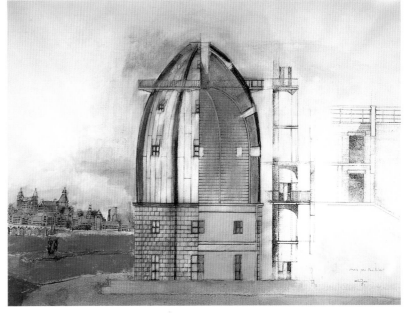

Top: Despite the strict, industrial appearance of the building, it functions well as a museum.
Left: The main entrance of the museum, with the Wiebengahal in the foreground, on the right.
Right: A plan of the museum, showing the dome at the top, and the Wiebengahal on the lower right.

Oben: Trotz der fast fabrikähnlich anmutenden Erscheinung wird das Gebäude seiner Funktion als Museum in jeder Weise gerecht.
Links: Eingangsbereich des Museums, mit der Wieben-gahal rechts im Vordergrund.
Rechts: Grundriß des Museums, mit der Kuppel im oberen Bildbereich und der Wiebengahal am unteren rechten Bildrand.

En haut: Malgré son aspect sévère et quasi-industriel, le bâtiment convient parfaitement à sa vocation muséale.
A gauche: L'entrée principale du musée, avec, au premier plan, le Wiebengahal, sur la droite.
A droite: Plan du musée, montrant le dôme, en haut, et le Wiebengahal, en bas à droite.

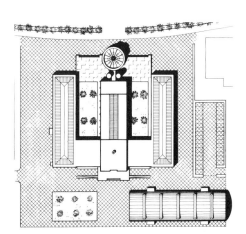

Right: The landing at the top of the monumental staircase. The internal detailing of the museum has been kept intentionally simple.
Above: The rapport with local industrial architecture is emphasized on the exterior as well.

Rechts: Das Podest am oberen Ende des monumentalen Treppenhauses. Die Inneneinrichtung des Museums wurde bewußt sehr schlicht gehalten.
Oben: Die enge Verbindung zur Industrie-Architektur der Umgebung zeigt sich auch bei der Gestaltung der Fassade.

A droite: Le palier, en haut de l'escalier monumental. Les détails intérieurs du musée restent volontairement sobres.
Ci-dessus: A l'extérieur aussi, le rapport avec l'architecture industrielle locale est accentué.

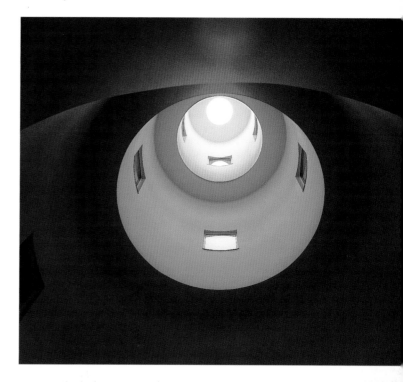

Page 138: The monumental staircase with its individually laid brick walls.
Bottom left: Two images showing the interior of the Wiebengahal, used to exhibit contemporary sculpture (top Willem de Kooning, bottom Richard Serra).

Seite 138: Das monumentale Treppenhaus mit seinen individuell gemauerten Ziegelsteinwänden.
Unten links: Zwei Innenansichten der Wiebengahal, die als Ausstellungsfläche für zeitgenössische Skulptur dient (oben Willem de Kooning, unten Richard Serra).

Page 138: L'escalier monumental, avec ses murs de briques posées une à une.
Ci-dessous à gauche: Deux images montrant l'intérieur du Wiebengahal, utilisé pour des expositions de sculptures contemporaines (en haut, Willem de Kooning, en bas, Richard Serra).

Top right: An image looking up the dome from the inside.
Bottom right: In the entrance to the museum in the axis of the monumental stairway, Rossi has placed a rather enigmatic circular volume which echoes the round form of the dome.

Oben rechts: Innenansicht der Kuppel.
Unten rechts: Im Eingangsbereich des Museums plazierte Rossi auf der Achse zum monumentalen Treppenhaus einen rätselhaften kreisförmigen Raum, der die runde Form der Kuppel noch einmal aufnimmt.

Ci-dessus à droite: Vue de la partie supérieure du dôme, prise de l'intérieur.
Ci-dessous à droite: A l'entrée du musée, dans l'axe de l'escalier monumental, Rossi a placé un volume circulaire plutôt énigmatique, qui reprend la forme ronde du dôme.

Aldo Rossi **139**

Schneider +
Schumacher

Still under 40 years of age, Till Schneider and Michael Schumacher, who both studied at the University of Kaiserslautern and at the Staatliche Hochschule für Bildende Künste, Städelschule, Frankfurt, in the class of Peter Cook, have succeeded in building a highly visible structure with their Info Box in the midst of the massive Leipziger-Potsdamer Platz construction area. Whereas Berlin's building plans provide for a very "solid" and perhaps staid architectural future, the Info Box seems to stand out as a signal that ephemeral forms can be more creative and amusing for visitors. Despite their youth, Schneider + Schumacher have completed a 5,915 m², 20 million DM office building for the J. Walter Thompson advertising agency on the Schwedlerstrasse in Frankfurt (1994–95), and are currently working on an administrative building on Beethovenstrasse in Leipzig, for the KPMG (Deutsche Treuhandgesellschaft). This 6,736 m², 17 million DM structure is expected to be ready for mid-1997.

Im Alter von unter vierzig Jahren gelang Till Schneider und Michael Schumacher – die beide an der Universität Kaiserslautern und in der Klasse von Peter Cook an der Staatlichen Hochschule für Bildende Künste, Städelschule, in Frankfurt studierten –, mit ihrer Info Box die Realisierung eines sehr auffälligen Bauwerkes mitten in Berlin, auf dem riesigen Baugelände des Leipziger-Potsdamer Platzes. Wo aufgrund der Berliner Planungen an einer sehr »soliden«, eher gesetzten architektonischen Zukunft gebaut wird, scheint die Info Box wie ein Zeichen dafür zu stehen, daß vergängliche Formen kreativer und für den Besucher amüsanter sein können. Trotz ihrer Jugend haben Schneider + Schumacher auf der Schwedlerstraße in Frankfurt bereits ein 5915 m² großes und 20 Millionen DM teures Bürogebäude für die Werbeagentur J. Walter Thompson fertiggestellt (1994–95) und arbeiten zur Zeit an einem Verwaltungsgebäude für die KPMG (Deutsche Treuhandgesellschaft), das auf der Beethovenstraße in Leipzig entsteht. Dieses 17 Millionen DM teure und 6736 m² große Gebäude soll Mitte 1997 fertiggestellt werden.

Till Schneider et Michael Schumacher ont moins de 40 ans. Ils ont tous les deux fait leurs études à l'université de Kaiserslautern et à la Staatliche Hochschule für Bildende Künste, Städelschule, à Francfort, avec Peter Cook. Située au milieu du chantier qui occupe l'immense Leipziger-Potsdamer Platz, leur Info Box est une construction bien visible. Tandis que les projets berlinois promettent à la ville un futur architectural très «massif» et quelque peu solennel, l'Info Box semble se détacher de cet ensemble comme pour montrer que des formes éphémères peuvent être plus créatives et plus amusantes pour les visiteurs. Malgré leur jeunesse, Schneider + Schumacher ont déjà réalisé un immeuble de bureaux de 5915 m² (1994–95; 20 millions de DM) pour l'agence de publicité J. Walter Thompson, située sur la Schwedlerstrasse, à Francfort. Ils construisent actuellement un bâtiment administratif pour la KPMG (Deutsche Treuhandgesellschaft), sur la Beethovenstrasse, à Leipzig. D'un coût global de 17 millions de DM, cet édifice de 6736 m² devrait être achevé vers la fin du premier semestre 1997.

Schneider + Schumacher, Info Box, Berlin, Germany, 1995. Detail.

Schneider + Schumacher, Info Box, Berlin, Deutschland, 1995. Detailansicht.

Schneider + Schumacher, Info Box, Berlin, Allemagne, 1995. Détail.

Info Box

Berlin, Germany, 1995

Built for a cost of 10 million Deutsche marks between June and October 1995, the Info Box is situated in the midst of the vast Potsdamer Platz work site. It was financed by partners in the project, with the intention of explaining future developments to the public. The building is 62.5 meters long, 15 meters wide and 23 meters high for a total area of 2,230 m². It is covered with 2500 x 500 mm wraparound red enameled weatherproof steel plates, and has "over-edge" glazing which permits views into and through the structure. The bottom platform, set up on 40 cm diameter concrete filled steel posts is seven meters above the ground. Given the extremely short construction time and limited budget, the architects opted for "rough" detailing, confirmed by the use of white gypsum boards and black linoleum flooring laid on timber boards inside the building. Intentionally ephemeral, the Info Box is meant to be dismantled when the buildings around it are completed, but it does seem esthetically well-suited to the apparently chaotic environment of the work site.

Die für 10 Millionen DM von Juni bis Oktober 1995 erbaute Info Box liegt inmitten der Großbaustelle Potsdamer Platz und soll die Öffentlichkeit über die zukünftigen Entwicklungen informieren. Das 62,5 Meter lange, 15 Meter breite und 23 Meter hohe Gebäude nimmt eine Gesamtfläche von 2230 m² ein. Es ist mit 2500 x 500 mm großen rotlackierten, wetterbeständigen Stahlblechen verkleidet, und besitzt sogenannte »Über-Eck-Verglasungen«, die den Blick in und durch den Bau hindurch ermöglichen. Die Bodenplattform ruht sieben Meter über der Erde auf betongefüllten Stahlrohren mit einem Durchmesser von 40 Zentimetern. Wegen der kurzen Bauzeit und begrenzter Baumittel entschieden sich die Architekten für ein »grobes« Finish, das durch die Verwendung von weißen Gipskartonplatten und dem auf den Holzbohlen der Innenräume ausgelegten schwarzen Linoleum-Bodenbelag unterstrichen wird. Die Info Box wurde bewußt als vergängliches Gebäude konzipiert und soll abgerissen werden, sobald die umliegenden Bauten fertiggestellt sind; ästhetisch paßt sie sich gut in das scheinbare Chaos der Großbaustellenumgebung ein.

Construite de juin à octobre 1995 pour un coût total de 10 millions de Deutsche marks, l'Info Box est située au milieu du chantier qui occupe la vaste Potsdamer Platz. Financé par divers partenaires, le projet est destiné à présenter au public les aménagements à venir. Le bâtiment fait 62,5 mètres de long, 15 mètres de large et 23 mètres de haut; il occupe une surface totale de 2230 m². Il est recouvert de plaques étanches de 2500 x 500 mm en acier émaillé rouge, et les nombreuses parois vitrées permettent de voir à travers la structure. La plate-forme inférieure repose sur des poteaux en acier de 40 cm de diamètre remplis de béton, sept mètres au-dessus du rez-de-chaussée. Etant donné les délais extrêmement courts et le budget limité, les architectes ont opté pour une finition intérieure «brute»: des murs en placoplâtre blanc et un sol en linoléum noir posé sur un plancher en bois de charpente. Volontairement éphémère, l'Info Box sera démantelée lorsque les bâtiments qui l'entourent seront achevés. Toutefois, son esthétique semble tout à fait adaptée à l'environnement apparemment chaotique du chantier.

Page 142 and 143 top: *Set in the midst of the Potsdamer Platz work site, near the site of the former Berlin
Wall, the Info Box appears to be a rather incongruous
object in part because of its bright red color.*
Page 143 bottom: *Set seven meters above the ground,
the Info Box seems as temporary as its present surroundings. A computer view shows how the Info Box
will look when the buildings around it are completed,
and before it is dismantled.*

Seite 142 und 143 oben: *Inmitten der Großbaustelle
Potsdamer Platz nahe der ehemaligen Berliner Mauer
scheint sich die Info Box schon wegen ihrer leuchtend
roten Farbe nicht in die Umgebung einzupassen.*
Seite 143 unten: *Das sieben Meter über Grund errichtete Gebäude wirkt so vergänglich wie seine Umgebung.
Eine Computergraphik zeigt die Info Box inmitten der
fertiggestellten umliegenden Bauwerke, bevor das
Gebäude abgerissen wird.*

Page 142 et Page 143 en haut: *Située au milieu du
chantier qui occupe la vaste Potsdamer Platz, près du
site de l'ancien Mur de Berlin, l'Info Box semble un
objet plutôt incongru, en partie à cause de son rouge vif.*
Page 143 en bas: *Juchée à sept mètres au-dessus du sol,
l'Info Box semble aussi éphémère que son environnement
actuel. Un dessin sur ordinateur montre à quoi elle
ressemblera quand les bâtiments alentour seront ter-
minés, et avant qu'elle ne soit démontée.*

The interior of the building is intentionally simple, with gypsum boards used for the walls in the exhibition area. An elevation and a floor plan express the fundamental simplicity of the structure.

Das Innere des Gebäudes wurde bewußt schlicht gehalten und besitzt im Ausstellungsbereich Trennwände aus Gipskartonplatten. Aufriß und Grundriß veranschaulichen die elementare Schlichtheit des Bauwerkes.

L'intérieur du bâtiment est volontairement simple avec, dans la zone d'exposition, des murs en placoplâtre blanc. Une élévation et un plan sol reflètent la simplicité fondamentale de la structure.

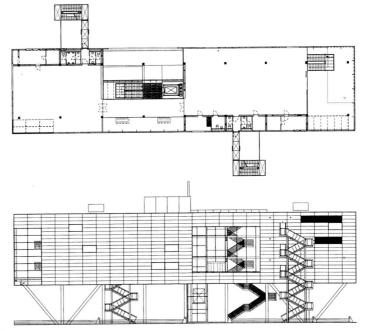

Schweger + Partner

It was after Heinz Graaf and Peter Schweger worked together designing the Fachhochschule (technical college) in Hamburg-Bergedorf in 1964 that they created an office together, and in 1968 the partnership Graaf + Schweger. This partnership was extended to include other principals as of 1973 and Architekten Schweger + Partner was created in 1987. Its principals today are Peter P. Schweger, Franz Wöhler, Hartmut H. Reifenstein, Bernhard Kohl and Wolfgang Schneider. The office of Schweger + Partner is a substantial one, with some 120 persons located in Hamburg, Hanover, Frankfurt, Berlin and Karlsruhe. They have participated in a large number of competitions, such as that for the Reichstag (1993), or the 1990 consultation for the Wolfsburg Museum which they built. They have built numerous office, commercial and residential buildings in Hamburg, Vienna or Munich; hotels in Vienna, Hamburg and Rostock; the "Sport Dome" in Hamburg; educational facilities in Hamburg and Hannover, and public buildings such as the Wolfsburg City Hall.

Nachdem Heinz Graaf und Peter Schweger 1964 beim Entwurf der Fachhochschule in Hamburg-Bergedorf zusammengearbeitet hatten, bezogen sie zusammen ein Büro, und 1968 entstand die Partnerschaft Graaf + Schweger. Ab 1973 erweiterte man das Büro um weitere Partner, bis 1987 Architekten Schweger + Partner entstand, dessen heutige Teilhaber Peter P. Schweger, Franz Wöhler, Hartmut H. Reifenstein, Bernhard Kohl und Wolfgang Schneider sind. Heute zählt das Büro Schweger + Partner nicht weniger als 120 Mitarbeiter und besitzt Niederlassungen in Hamburg, Hannover, Frankfurt, Berlin und Karlsruhe. Schweger + Partner beteiligten sich an einer Reihe von Architekturwettbewerben, darunter auch für den Reichstag (1993) und das Kunstmuseum Wolfsburg, den sie 1990 gewannen. Darüber hinaus erbauten sie zahlreiche Büro-, Geschäfts- und Wohnhäuser in Hamburg, München und Wien, Hotels in Wien, Hamburg und Rostock, den »Sport Dome« in Hamburg, Unterrichtsstätten in Hamburg und Hannover und öffentliche Gebäude wie das Wolfsburger Rathaus.

Après avoir collaboré à la conception de la Fachhochschule (établissement d'enseignement technique) de Hambourg-Bergedorf en 1964, Heinz Graaf et Peter Schweger ont créé ensemble une agence, puis se sont associés en 1968. A partir de 1973, cette association s'élargit pour inclure d'autres partenaires et Architekten Schweger + Partner est créé en 1987. Aujourd'hui, on y trouve Peter P. Schweger, Franz Wöhler, Hartmut H. Reifenstein, Bernhard Kohl et Wolfgang Schneider. L'agence Schweger + Partner compte quelque 120 personnes travaillant à Hambourg, Hanovre, Francfort, Berlin et Karlsruhe. Ses membres ont participé à de nombreux concours – comme celui du Reichstag (1993) – et à la consultation de 1990 organisée pour le musée de Wolfsburg, qu'ils ont finalement construit. Ils ont conçu de nombreux immeubles commerciaux et résidentiels à Hambourg, Vienne et Munich; des hôtels à Vienne, Hambourg et Rostock; le «Sport Dome» de Hambourg; des équipements scolaires à Hambourg et à Hanovre; des édifices publics, dont l'hôtel de ville de Wolfsburg.

Schweger + Partner, Kunstmuseum Wolfsburg, Wolfsburg, Germany, 1989–93. Ramp and roof detail.

Schweger + Partner, Kunstmuseum Wolfsburg, Wolfsburg, Deutschland, 1989–93. Detailansicht der Rampe und der Dachkonstruktion.

Schweger + Partner, Kunstmuseum de Wolfsburg, Wolfsburg, Allemagne, 1989–93. Rampe et détail du toit.

Kunstmuseum Wolfsburg
Wolfsburg, Germany, 1989–1993

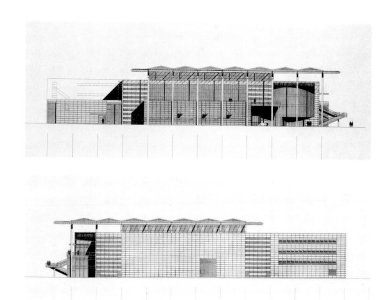

Funded by the Volkswagen Art Foundation, this new museum is intended to fit into the city's urban master plan, reinterpreting the southern entrance to city center in relation to existing buildings such as the Kulturzentrum designed by Alvar Aalto in 1962 and Hans Scharoun's 1973 theater. An 8,510 m² building with 3,500 m² set aside for exhibitions the building is laid out along the lines of a 8.10 x 8.10 meter primary grid subdivided into 1.35 meter bays corresponding with the articulation of the facade and the roof. The granite of the square in front of the entrance is also used inside the building, and the canopy-like 18.8 meter high grated steel truss roof sweeps out to the north and west over exterior areas. The entrance rotunda is 16.8 meters high. A sophisticated new type of micro-grid "consisting of plastic surfaces vapor-coated with pure aluminum reflects the angular portion of direct sunlight into the atmosphere," assuring a natural overhead lighting well suited to the display of works of art.

Page 148: Elevations give an idea of the geometric grid which govern the forms of the building. The extension of the roof over the entrance rotunda is also evident in the drawings. Page 149: Inside the rotunda, the granite paving also used outside accentuates the impression of openness.

Seite 148: Die Aufrisse vermitteln einen Eindruck des geometrischen Rasters, das die Form des Gebäudes beherrscht. Die Dacherweiterung oberhalb der Eingangsrotunde ist auch auf den Zeichnungen zu sehen. Seite 149: Im Inneren des Rundbaus akzentuiert die auch im Außenbereich verwendete Granitpflasterung den Eindruck von Offenheit und Weite.

Page 148: Les élévations donnent une idée du quadrillage géométrique qui gouverne les formes du bâtiment. L'extension du toit, au-dessus de la rotonde d'entrée est également visible sur les dessins. Page 149: A l'intérieur de la rotonde, l'impression d'ouverture est accentuée par le dallage en granit qui se poursuit à l'extérieur.

Das neue, von der Volkswagen-Stiftung finanzierte Museum wurde so konzipiert, daß es sich in den Stadtbebauungsplan einpaßt. Zusammen mit bereits bestehenden Gebäuden wie dem 1962 von Alvar Aalto entworfenen Kulturzentrum und Hans Scharouns Stadttheater von 1973 soll es dem südlichen Zugang zum Stadtzentrum ein neues Gesicht verleihen. Das Gebäude besitzt eine Gesamtfläche von 8510 m², von der 3500 m² für Ausstellungen vorgesehen sind. Es wurde auf einem in 8,10 x 8,10 Meter große Flächen eingeteilten übergeordneten Raster konzipiert, das wiederum in Felder von 1,35 Meter unterteilt ist, die der Gliederung von Fassade und Dach entsprechen. Die Granitpflasterung des Platzes vor dem Eingang findet auch im Gebäudeinneren Verwendung, und das einem Baldachin ähnelnde, 18,8 Meter hohe und mit Stahlgitterträgern versteifte Dach springt nach Norden und Westen hin weit über das umliegende Gelände vor. Die Eingangsrotunde hat eine Höhe von 16,8 Metern. Ein neuartiger, raffinierter Mikrogitterrost, »der aus Kunststoffoberflächen mit aufgedampfter Reinaluminiumbeschichtung besteht, wirft das schräg einfallende Sonnenlicht in die Atmosphäre zurück« und schafft so eine Beleuchtung durch von oben einfallendes Tageslicht, die sich gut für die Ausstellung von Kunstobjekten eignet.

Financé par la Fondation d'art Volkswagen, ce nouveau musée est conçu de façon à s'intégrer au plan d'urbanisme de Wolfsburg et à redéfinir l'entrée sud de la ville par rapport à des bâtiments existants tels que le Kulturzentrum construit par Alvar Aalto en 1962 et le théâtre conçu par Hans Scharoun en 1973. Cet édifice de 8510 m² (dont 3500 m² de surface d'exposition) est conçu à partir d'un quadrillage de base de 8,10 x 8,10 mètres subdivisé en baies de 1,35 mètres correspondant à l'articulation de la façade et du toit. L'architecte a utilisé le même granit sur la place située devant l'entrée et à l'intérieur du bâtiment. Le toit se prolonge par un immense auvent à armature d'acier posé à 18,8 m au-dessus du sol et qui forme des grands espaces ouverts/couverts devant les façades nord et ouest du musée. La rotonde située à l'entrée s'élève à 16,8 mètres. Un nouveau type sophistiqué de micro-quadrillage «composé de surfaces en plastique recouvertes d'une pellicule d'aluminium pur reflète dans l'atmosphère la portion angulaire de rayons de soleil directs». L'éclairage zénithal naturel qui en résulte convient tout à fait à la présentation d'œuvres d'art.

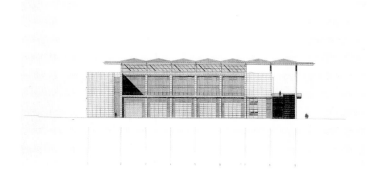

Pages 150/151: *The thinness of the extending roof and of its supporting columns give a feeling of lightness to the structure, as well as adding, like the access ramp, to the perceived and real permeability of the Kunstmuseum.*

Seite 150/151: *Die Feinheit des vorkragenden Daches und seiner tragenden Stützen verleiht dem Gebäude den Eindruck von Leichtigkeit und Transparenz und betont – ebenso wie die Zugangsrampe – die sowohl augenscheinliche als auch tatsächliche Durchlässigkeit des Kunstmuseums.*

Pages 150/151: *La légèreté du toit en auvent et des colonnes qui le soutiennent donne au bâtiment une grâce aérienne qui, tout comme la rampe d'accès, renforce l'aspect accueillant et ouvert du Kunstmuseum.*

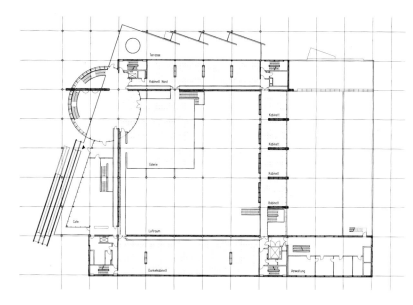

In some contemporary structures, high ceilings and generous spaces are reserved for entrance foyers. This is obviously not the case in Wolfsburg, where an emphasis on structural flexibility permits the display of works of considerable dimensions.

Bei vielen modernen Bauwerken sind hohe Decken und großzügige Räume dem Eingangsbereich vorbehalten – was in Wolfsburg ganz eindeutig nicht der Fall ist, da man beim Kunstmuseum Wert auf strukturelle Flexibilität legte, die auch die Ausstellung großformatiger Kunstwerke ermöglicht.

Dans certaines structures contemporaines, les hauts plafonds et les espaces généreux sont réservés au foyer d'accueil. A l'évidence, ce n'est pas le cas à Wolfsburg, où l'accent est mis sur la flexibilité de la structure et permet d'exposer des œuvres monumentales.

Schweger + Partner **153**

Night views emphasize the transparency of the building, and in particular of the roof and entrance rotunda areas. Despite the rigorous application of the grid system, and a relatively "High-Tech" approach, the impression of lightness and openness dominates.

Nachtansichten beweisen die Transparenz des Gebäudes – insbesondere des Daches sowie der Eingangsrotunde. Ungeachtet der rigorosen Anwendung des Rastersystems und der »High-Tech«-Bezüge entstand ein Gesamteindruck von Leichtigkeit und Weite.

Ces vues nocturnes soulignent la transparence du bâtiment, en particulier celle du toit et de la rotonde à l'entrée. Malgré l'application rigoureuse de ce quadrillage et une approche plutôt «high-tech», une impression de légèreté et d'ouverture prédomine.

Alvaro Siza

Situated somewhere between contemporary trends toward mannerist and rationalist approaches, most of Alvaro Siza's buildings have a relatively simple appearance, with long, flat surfaces, yet their plans, and some of their details are in fact quite complex. Born in 1933, winner of the 1992 Pritzker Prize, Siza has had a decisive influence on recent Portuguese architecture. His respectful approach to problems of context has not precluded the creation of forceful, modern buildings. As he has written, "We change space as we change ourselves – by pieces, confronted with *the other* collectively and individually. Nature, the abode of man, and man, the creator of Nature, both absorb everything, embodying or rejecting it in a transitory way, as everything leaves its mark on them. Departing from isolated pieces, we search the space that bears the pieces."

Alvaro Sizas Gebäude sind irgendwo zwischen den zeitgenössischen Trends zur manieristischen bzw. zur rationalistischen Architektur angesiedelt. Sie besitzen ein relativ schlichtes Erscheinungsbild mit langgestreckten, glatten Oberflächen, aber einige ihrer Details sind äußerst komplex. Der 1933 geborene Siza, Gewinner des Pritzker Preis 1992, übt entscheidenden Einfluß auf die zeitgenössische portugiesische Architektur aus. Sein respektvoller Umgang mit den Problemen des jeweiligen Kontextes hat ihn nicht vom Bau kraftvoller, moderner Gebäude abgehalten. Siza schreibt: »Wir verändern den Raum, wie wir uns selbst verändern – in einzelnen Teilen, wobei wir mit dem *Anderen* im Kollektiv und als Individuen konfrontiert werden. Die Natur, der Wohnort des Menschen, und der Mensch, der Gestalter der Natur – beide absorbieren alles, nehmen es auf flüchtige Weise in sich auf oder stoßen es von sich ab, wobei alles seine Spuren auf ihnen hinterläßt. Ausgehend von einzelnen Teilen suchen wir den Raum, der die Teile in sich schließt.«

Situés quelque part entre les courants maniéristes contemporains et les approches rationalistes, la plupart des bâtiments d'Alvaro Siza offrent un aspect relativement simple, avec des surfaces longues et planes. Toutefois, leur plan et certains détails sont en réalité très complexes. Né en 1933 et lauréat du prix Pritzker en 1992, Siza a eu une influence décisive sur l'architecture portugaise de ces dernières années. Son approche respectueuse des problèmes de contexte ne l'a pas empêché de créer des bâtiments vigoureux et modernes. «Nous modifions l'espace comme nous nous modifions nous-mêmes, par morceaux, confrontés à ‹l'autre› collectivement et individuellement. La nature, demeure de l'homme, et l'homme, créateur de la nature, absorbent tout. Ils incarnent et rejettent tout de façon passagère, tandis que chaque chose laisse sa marque sur eux. A partir de morceaux isolés, nous cherchons l'espace qui contient ces morceaux.»

Alvaro Siza, Galician Center for Contemporary Art, Santiago de Compostela, Spain, 1988–95. The intersection of the old and the new.

Alvaro Siza, Galizisches Zentrum für zeitgenössische Kunst, Santiago de Compostela, Spanien, 1988–95. Durchdringung von Altem und Neuem.

Alvaro Siza, Centre galicien d'art contemporain, Saint-Jacques-de-Compostelle, Espagne, 1988–95. La rencontre de l'ancien et du nouveau.

Galician Center for Contemporary Art
Santiago de Compostela, Spain, 1988–1995

This 7,000 m² museum building is set on a triangular lot in the midst of the 17th century Santo Domingo de Bonaval convent. Clad in granite like many local buildings, it seeks to respond in a modern, yet appropriate way to its surroundings, and even to give greater harmony to the existing group of historic structures in its immediate environment. Siza says, "I can't say exactly why, but I am convinced, because I have visited Santiago intensively, that the building seems very natural in this urban landscape." Its long, often blank facades respond to the nearby rough stone walls. As the architect points out, there were neither collections nor a curator when he received this commission, requiring him to set out a flexible solution which he found in the shape of a plan made up of two overlapping L-shaped volumes. Both on the outside, and within, an emphasis has been placed on a purity of line. The white interiors, with Greek marble flooring in the public areas are rendered all the more pure through a suspended ceiling, concealing security systems and lighting.

Das 7000 m² große Museumsgebäude liegt auf einer dreieckigen Bauparzelle mitten im Kloster Santo Domingo de Bonaval, das aus dem 17. Jahrhundert stammt. Bei dem Museum, das wie viele Gebäude der Gegend mit Granit verkleidet ist, wurde nicht nur versucht, in moderner, aber angemessener Art auf die Umgebung einzugehen, sondern zudem eine größere Harmonie innerhalb einer Gruppe umliegender historischer Bauten angestrebt. Siza erklärt dazu: »Ich kann keine genauen Gründe dafür nennen, aber ich bin nach intensiven Studien in Santiago davon überzeugt, daß das Gebäude im Gesamtbild dieser Stadt sehr natürlich wirkt.« Die langgestreckten, nahezu undurchbrochenen Fassaden des Museums korrespondieren mit den benachbarten Steinmauern. Wie der Architekt erläutert, gab es zu dem Zeitpunkt, als er den Auftrag für das Museum erhielt, weder eine Sammlung noch einen Museumsdirektor, so daß eine flexible Lösung gefragt war. Eine solche Lösung fand er in dem Entwurf zweier L-förmiger, einander überschneidender Baukörper. Sowohl außen als auch innen wurde Nachdruck auf die Klarheit der Linien gelegt. Durch die abgehängte Decke, hinter der sich Sicherheitssysteme und Beleuchtung verbergen, wirken die in Weiß gehaltenen Innenräume mit Fußböden aus griechischem Marmor in den öffentlich zugänglichen Bereichen noch makelloser.

Ce musée de 7000 m² est construit sur un terrain triangulaire situé au cœur du couvent Santo Domingo de Bonaval, qui date du XVIIe siècle. Revêtu de granit à l'image de nombreux édifices locaux, il entend cohabiter avec ce qui l'entoure de façon moderne mais cohérente. Il cherche même à apporter plus d'harmonie à l'ensemble d'édifices historiques situé dans son environnement immédiat. «Je suis incapable de dire exactement pourquoi, dit Siza, mais je suis convaincu – parce que j'ai tellement visité Saint-Jacques – que la présence de ce bâtiment paraît très naturelle dans ce paysage urbain.» Les façades longues et pour la plupart aveugles du musée font écho aux murs de pierre voisins. Comme le fait remarquer l'architecte, au moment où il a reçu cette commande, il n'y avait pas encore de collections ni de conservateur, ce qui l'a obligé à rechercher une solution souple. Ainsi, il a conçu un plan constitué de deux volumes en forme de L se recouvrant partiellement. A l'intérieur comme à l'extérieur, l'accent a été mis sur la pureté des lignes. Le sol des zones publiques est couvert de marbre grec, et la blancheur des salles est rendue encore plus pure grâce à un plafond suspendu qui masque les systèmes de sécurité et d'éclairage.

Alvaro Siza was fascinated by the Baroque monastery facade, which influenced his choice of almost blank granite walls. The tour of the GCCA logically ends on the rooftop which affords a view of the surrounding buildings, and the city. It is intended for the exhibition of sculpture.

Alvaro Sizas Begeisterung für die Fassade des Barockklosters beeinflußte ihn in seiner Entscheidung für nahezu undurchbrochene Granitwände. Der Weg durch das GCCA endet auf dem Dach des Gebäudes, von wo aus sich der Blick auf die umliegenden Gebäude und die Stadt bietet. Dieser Teil soll als Ausstellungsfläche für Skulpturen dienen.

Alvaro Siza a été fasciné par la façade du monastère baroque qui l'a influencé dans son choix de murs de granit, presque aveugles. Logiquement, la visite du CGAC se termine par le toit qui offre une vue sur les bâtiments alentour et la ville. Il est destiné à des expositions de sculptures.

The plan of the museum is constituted by two L-shaped volumes. Inverted and overlapping, these elements give a rich variety of internal and external geometric compositions. The interiors are intentionally free of protruding elements such as track lighting or security devices, which have been hidden, mostly in the ceiling.

Der Grundriß des Museums setzt sich aus zwei L-förmigen Baukörpern zusammen, die einander überschneiden und damit eine große Vielfalt interner und externer geometrischer Kompositionen ermöglichen. Die Innenräume wurden bewußt von hervorstehenden Elementen wie Lichtschienen oder Sicherheitssystemen frei gehalten, die – für den Betrachter unsichtbar – hauptsächlich hinter der Deckenverkleidung verlaufen.

Le plan du musée est constitué de deux volumes en forme de L. Inversés et se recouvrant partiellement, ces éléments permettent une grande diversité de compositions géométriques. L'intérieur est volontairement exempt de tout élément saillant, tels que rampes d'éclairage, ou systèmes de sécurité, essentiellement dissimulés dans le plafond.

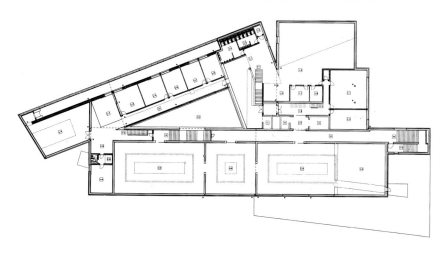

Valode & Pistre

The work of Denis Valode and Jean Pistre is varied, but often on a large scale, and usually obtained through participation in competitions. In recent years, their office has employed between 45 and 80 persons, which in France is considered to be a large number. They have recently begun to participate in competitions outside of France, such as that for the renovation of the souk of Beirut which they won in 1994. Valode & Pistre attempt, as was the case with their L'Oréal factory in Aulnay-sous-Bois, to maintain a personalized approach combined with industrial methods. They reject both the "star system" of contemporary architecture and the opposing tendency to highly commercial, repetitive work, which has led them to work as different as the renovation of warehouses in Bordeaux to create a contemporary art center (CAPC, 1990) and to the more functional offices of Air France at Roissy (1992–95).

Die Bauprojekte von Denis Valode und Jean Pistre sind sehr verschiedenartig, meist in großem Maßstab gehalten und werden im allgemeinen durch die Teilnahme an Wettbewerben eingeholt. In den letzten Jahren beschäftigte ihr Büro zwischen 45 und 80 Mitarbeitern, eine für französische Verhältnisse große Zahl. Seit kurzem beteiligen sich Valode & Pistre auch an Wettbewerben außerhalb Frankreichs, wie etwa im Falle der Neugestaltung des Souk von Beirut, dessen Wettbewerb sie 1994 gewannen. Valode & Pistre streben, wie bei den von ihnen erbauten L'Oréal-Werken in Aulnay-sous-Bois, nach einem persönlichen Architekturansatz, den sie mit industriellen Methoden kombinieren. Beide lehnen das »Star-System« der zeitgenössischen Architekturszene ebenso ab wie die entgegengesetzte Tendenz zu hochkommerziellen, repetitiven Bauprojekten – was dazu führte, daß sie so unterschiedliche Projekte wie den Umbau eines Warenhauses in Bordeaux zu einem Zentrum für zeitgenössische Kunst (CAPC, 1990) ebenso betreuen wie den Bau funktioneller Büros für die Air France in Roissy (1992–95).

Le travail de Denis Valode et Jean Pistre se caractérise par sa diversité. Ils travaillent essentiellement sur des projets à grande échelle, le plus souvent remportés par concours. Ces dernières années, leur agence a employé entre 45 et 80 personnes, ce qui est considéré en France comme un nombre important. Depuis peu, ils participent à des concours à l'étranger, comme celui qu'ils ont remporté en 1994 pour la rénovation du souk de Beyrouth. Comme l'illustre l'exemple de l'usine L'Oréal d'Aulnay-sous-Bois, Valode & Pistre essaient de garder une approche personnalisée associée à des méthodes industrielles. Ils rejettent tous les deux le «vedettariat» de l'architecture contemporaine et la tendance opposée qui consiste à proposer un travail très commercial et répétitif. Cette attitude les a amenés à travailler sur des projets aussi différents que la rénovation d'entrepôts bordelais en vu de créer un centre d'art contemporain (CAPC, 1990) ou la construction plus fonctionnelle de bureaux pour Air France à Roissy (1992–95).

Valode & Pistre, L'Oréal Factory, Aulnay-sous-Bois, France, 1988–91. Detail showing glass wall.

Valode & Pistre, L'Oréal-Werke, Aulnay-sous-Bois, Frankreich, 1988–91. Detailansicht der Glaswand.

Valode & Pistre, L'usine L'Oréal, Aulnay-sous-Bois, France, 1988–91. Détail du mur en verre.

L'Oréal Factory
Aulnay-sous-Bois, France, 1988–1991

The most spectacular, and visible feature of this 30,000 m² manufacturing and administrative complex for a cosmetics firm located in the Paris region, is its three-petaled aluminum/polyethylene (Alucobon) roof. The upper roofing, designed with the assistance of the late engineer Peter Rice is composed of 7,023 elements set on partitions attached to galvanized steel pins. Because of the complex curvature involved, Rice's armature of inverted pyramids conceived to sustain the roof had to be designed to receive and concentrate forces applied from 14 axial directions, a task which could only be accomplished with the assistance of computers. 655 different families of lacquered panels were installed one by one at four points. The height of the panels was calculated in the architects' office, then on the site, a computer and a laser guided checking system, were used to make more than 21,000 on-site adjustments. The petal structure permits the creation of free interior platforms measuring 130 x 60 meters with neither pillars nor columns.

Auffallendstes und sichtbarstes Merkmal dieses 30 000 m² großen Produktions- und Verwaltungskomplexes eines Kosmetikherstellers in der Nähe von Paris ist das drei Blütenblättern nachempfundene Dach aus Aluminium-Polyäthylen (Alucobon). Die in Zusammenarbeit mit dem verstorbenen Ingenieur Peter Rice entworfene obere Bedachung besteht aus 7023 Elementen, die an Paneelen angebracht wurden, die ihrerseits an galvanisierten Stahlstiften befestigt sind. Aufgrund der komplizierten Krümmung mußte die von Rice entworfene Verstärkung aus umgekehrten Pyramiden, die das Dach trägt, so konstruiert werden, daß sie aus 14 Axialrichtungen einwirkende Kräfte auffangen und ableiten kann. Diese Aufgabe ließ sich nur mit Einsatz von Computern bewältigen. 655 unterschiedliche Gruppen lackierter Platten wurden einzeln und nacheinander an vier Punkten montiert. Die Höhe der Platten war zunächst im Architekturbüro kalkuliert worden; später nahm man vor Ort mit Hilfe eines Computers und eines Laser-Prüfsystems über 21 000 Anpassungen vor. Die Blütenblattkonstruktion ermöglichte es, im Gebäudeinnern freie, bis zu 130 x 60 Meter große Plattformen ohne Pfeiler oder Stützen einzuziehen.

Situé en région parisienne, ce complexe de 30 000 m² regroupe les chaînes de fabrication et les locaux administratifs d'une firme de cosmétiques. La caractéristique la plus spectaculaire et la plus visible de cet ouvrage est son toit en aluminium et polyéthylène (Alucobon) évoquant trois pétales. Conçue avec l'aide de Peter Rice, ingénieur disparu depuis, la partie supérieure de la toiture est composée de 7023 éléments fixés sur des panneaux maintenus par des goujons en acier galvanisé. En raison de la complexité de la courbure, l'armature composée de pyramides inversées destinée à soutenir le toit devait être conçue de manière à recevoir et à concentrer les forces appliquées depuis 14 directions axiales. Ce travail de conception ne pouvait être accompli sans l'aide de l'informatique. 655 séries de panneaux laqués ont été installées une par une en quatre points différents. La hauteur des panneaux a été calculée dans les bureaux d'étude, puis, sur le site, on a utilisé un ordinateur et un système de vérification par laser pour réaliser plus de 21 000 ajustements sur le terrain. La structure en pétales permet la création de plates-formes intérieures mobiles mesurant 130 x 60 m, sans piliers ni colonnes.

Set in a rather unattractive area on the periphery of Paris, the L'Oréal Factory is best understood in the plan to the left and the aerial views to the right which reveal the elegant tripartite structure, enclosing the central garden.

Die in einem eher unattraktiven Areal am Stadtrand von Paris gelegenene Fabrik der Firma L'Oréal erschließt sich dem Betrachter am besten anhand des Grundrisses (links) und der Luftaufnahmen (rechts), die die elegante, dreiteilige Konstruktion zeigt, welche wiederum den Garten in der Mitte umschließt.

Située dans un site peu attractif, à la périphérie de Paris, l'Usine l'Oréal peut mieux être comprise, grâce à ce plan (à gauche) et à cette vues aériennes (à droite) qui révèle son élégante structure tripartite, autour du jardin central.

Right: Valode & Pistre have been particularly successful in offering an unusually bright and spacious working area in this factory. The central garden accentuates the idea of a pleasant workplace.
Left, above and below: Structural details, including one of the nodes of the space frame superstructure.
Pages 168/169: The central garden which is almost entirely enclosed by the spectacular sloping roofs of the three "petals"

Rechts: Valode & Pistre gelang es, die Fabrik mit einem außergewöhnlich lichten und geräumigen Werksgelände zu versehen. Der zentrale Garten betont die Vorstellung eines angenehmen Arbeitsumfeldes.
Links, oben und unten: Strukturelle Details, einschließlich eines Knotenpunkts des räumlichen Tragwerkes.**Seite 168/169:** Der zentrale Garten, der fast vollständig von den geneigten Dächern der drei »Blütenblätter« umschlossen wird.

A droite: Valode & Pistre ont magistralement réussi à créer une zone de travail spacieuse et particulièrement claire. Le jardin central accentue l'idée de lieu agréable.
A gauche, ci-dessus et ci-dessous: Détails, y compris un point nodal de la superstructure.
Pages 168/169: Le jardin central, presque totalement encerclé par les toits qui s'abaissent majestueusement et forment les trois «pétales».

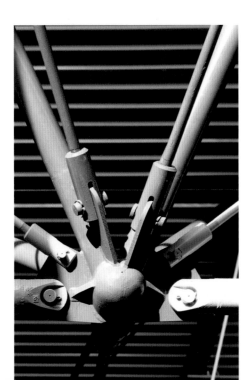